THE ACCOMPLISHING MORE WITH LESS

WORKBOOK

Pierre Khawand

Table of Contents

Introduction

Welcome to the Accomplishing More With Less Workbook. Join us in making the workplace less hectic and interruption-driven, more satisfying and results-driven instead. We work and live in an era of interruptions. The very moment you begin a task, you are stopped by emails, IMs, colleague visits, phone calls, meetings, and now, tweets and Facebook updates. The very technologies that were invented to enhance productivity have made it nearly impossible to get work done. Not only this, we are bombarded by an unprecedented information overload dominated by the Internet and globalization. This puts unreasonable demands on our work and personal lives, and as a result, we suffer, feel helpless, and our accomplishments decline. This needs to stop!

As a result of a decade of research and teaching on corporate and academic campuses, in person and virtually via web and video conferencing, my key findings about how to overcome the challenges of the information overload and accomplish meaningful things have been incorporated into the Accomplishing More With Less Workshop and in this Workbook. Thousands of participants have made significant breakthroughs using the Accomplishing More With Less (AML) Methodology and you can too!

What will you be able to do as a result?

- Better manage interruptions and stay focused on the task on hand until meaningful results are achieved while being responsive to the demands of your team and collaborate more effectively than ever before.

- Work more strategically instead of working harder, methodically manage competing priorities, and learn new and innovative tools that can help you better align your daily activities with your goals.

- Organize and manage your electronic and paper information easily and efficiently via a duplicate process that is practical and doable, instead of having your day "run over" by information and "low impact" activities.

- Manage stress like never before through purposeful action rather than passive reaction and turn stressful situations into opportunities.

- Understand the obstacles that are stopping you from reaching your desired accomplishments, and take the necessary actions that will lead to growth and transformation, and significantly increased fulfillment.

The Workshop in a Book

While this workbook is designed for the Accomplishing More With Less Workshop participants, it is also the "workshop in a book" for those who cannot join us live. It includes the AML concepts and workshop exercises, which you can follow on your own.

Becoming Certified

Just as importantly, this workbook enables independent and internal trainers, coaches, HR Professionals, and functional managers, to become certified to teach or use the Accomplishing More With Less (AML) Methodology in their own programs and help their clients or internal teams develop valuable skills and overcome the challenges of the information overload. For more information on how to get certified, training@people-onthego.com

Gift Certificate Included – for an Online Live Workshop

When you buy this book (whether to attend the People-OnTheGo workshop or a workshop through one of our certified partners), you are entitled to a gift certificate that enables you to attend one of our online workshops for a nominal registration fee of $10 (the regular fees for these workshops are either $69 or $99). These workshops cover topics such as:

- Managing and Organizing Your E-mail Inbox Using Outlook

- Total Organization

- Microsoft Excel Techniques – taking your skills to the next level

- Advanced Excel PivotTables

- Advanced Excel Macros

- Microsoft Word Techniques – taking your skills to the next level

- Microsoft PowerPoint Techniques – taking your skills to the next level

- Microsoft SharePoint Techniques – collaboration at its best

- Blogs, wikis, and SharePoint – collaboration in action

- And more!

    The complete schedule of public workshops is available at: www.people-onthego.com/public_workshops.html

    To claim your gift certificate, please e-mail the proof of purchase of your workbook (the online receipt) to training@people-onthego.com and include "Workbook gift certificate" in the subject line. You have 6 months to claim your gift certificate and attend your online workshop after the purchase of the workbook.

How to Get the Most Out Of This Workbook

Workshop participants will be guided through the methodology and the workbook exercises during the actual workshop. If, however, you are going through this workbook on your own, to really experience a transformation, we recommend that you treat it like a 'live' workshop and go through it at a pre-determined pace – such as one or two chapters per day or per week depending on your schedule, while doing the exercises along the way. We retain 10 to 20% of what we hear, 30% of what we see, and 70 to 90% of what we do. So doing is key.

Throughout the workbook, you will be asked to try new techniques. We invite you to try each technique whole-heartedly with the mindset of a curious learner. This will give you the opportunity to get new insights and expand your perspective. Then you can make an informed decision as to whether to incorporate the new technique into your daily work, or tailor it to fit your needs, or let go of it.

If you cannot go through the exercises as described above, you can still get plenty of insights by simply reading the workbook or just referring to the topics that are of interest to you right now. Then you can visit other topics when they become more relevant and applicable to your needs. This "on an as-needed basis approach" is one of the concepts we promote in the Accomplishing More With Less Methodology. This approach can help us get started and reap immediate benefits instead of waiting for the right time to come and prolonging the current challenges and less-than-optimum conditions.

How to stay in touch

We invite you to join us and become part of the Accomplishing More With Less community, which includes thousands of professionals who want to be more effective and more fulfilled at work and beyond, as well as contribute more fully to their organizations and to their communities. Here are ways in which you can become part of this community:

- Join the "Accomplishing more with less group" on Facebook

- Join the "Accomplishing more with less group" on LinkedIn

- Join our complimentary lunch & learn webinars every Thursday at noon Pacific Time. See the full program and registration information at:

  www.people-onthego.com/lunchandlearn-ontheair.html

- Connect with me on Twitter (@pierrekhawand)

Congratulations

Congratulations for choosing to be part of the Accomplishing More With Less movement. Your exciting and fulfilling journey has just begun!

Chapter 1: The Myth of Multitasking—focus to get results

The digital revolution should make us all incredibly efficient and productive. The tools at our fingertips — easy multimedia production software, instant and free communication around the globe, massive research power without needing to get up out of our chair — should allow us to complete tasks in hours instead of days and leave us more leisure time than we could ever have imagined. And yet this promise of efficiency seems to be just a little beyond where we are right now, somehow always eluding our grip. We can't seem to get there.

Our work environment is one of great onslaught. We struggle to get done on Friday what we had hoped to achieve the previous Monday. Why is it so difficult to do the things we really want to do? Keep on reading!

The Results Curve™

Let us start by examining how our results change with time when we are working on a task. In an ideal world, when we start to work on a task, we start to produce results, and then as we continue to work on that task, we produce more results. This continues until eventually the flow of results begins to level off and start to diminish. Results diminish because we get tired or saturated, or because we have done what we could and now need to wait for someone else to do their part, or because we have completed the task. The graph below (the Results Curve™) illustrates this progression:

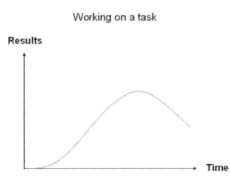

Now let's get back to *real* life. What happens in the real world after we spend a few minutes on a task?

We get interrupted!

E-mail arrives in our inbox and we feel this irresistible urge to check it out, or an instant message (IM) pops up with a compelling proposition. Then there's the phone ringing or a chatty colleague or eager boss stopping by. When an interruption takes place, it prematurely ends the progress on the task at hand as shown in the graph below:

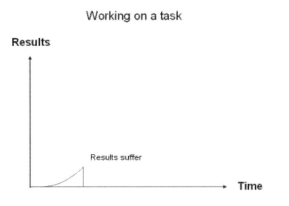

Post-interruption, when we resume our work on this task, are we going to start at the same level where we left off? Unfortunately not! Our mind needs to re-retrieve the relevant pieces of information that were let go of during the interruption and reconstruct the logic and relationships that were previously established. This means we will suffer a setback at the restarting point as shown below.

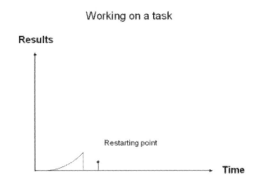

We start making progress again, but a few minutes later, another interruption pulls us off task, and our results suffer again:

Working on a task

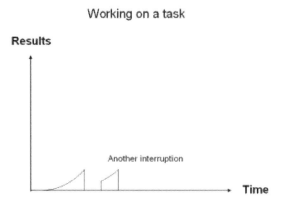

This pattern repeats itself time after time as the calls, emails, and IM's continue. Interruptions are no longer the exceptions in the digital age – they are the norm. The graph below illustrates this phenomenon. This is our life: a life of interruptions.

Working on a task

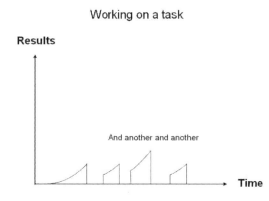

A Life of Interruptions

If we compare the actual results that we are getting, represented by the shaded areas in the graph below, to the potential results that we could realize if we could manage to focus on one task, represented by that beautiful uninterrupted Results Curve™, the outcome is nothing less than shocking:

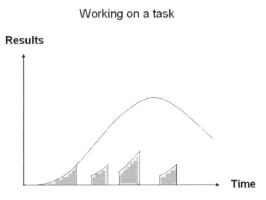

Working on a task

Our life has become a series of frequent interruptions intermingled with small bursts of work in which our ability to achieve anything of quality has been highly diluted. We are preventing ourselves from reaching the potential results area in the graph by letting interruptions take us off track and deprive us from using our gifts.

The Myth of Multi-Tasking

While some of us take pride in our ability to handle multiple tasks at the same time, and even believe that we are actually accomplishing more as we multitask, in reality there is no such a thing as true multi-tasking when it comes to the human mind. What we are really doing is task switching. Yes, some of us who are highly gifted can walk and chew gum at the same time. But those are autonomous functions — something that goes on in the autonomous part of our nervous system. It's our brain's ability to digest our food without asking us to think about it, or the part that keeps us breathing even though we're fast asleep. But when it comes to the limitations of our conscious brain, we cannot do two demanding things at once. Sorry, but there it is.

The cost of task switching is immense. In addition to the tangible cost of time, and the less tangible but significant opportunity cost, we also suffer individually and collectively from increased stress and less than satisfying work conditions as we race from one thing to another all day long and generally feel at the end of the day that we haven't actually accomplished much at all.

The Accomplishment Zone™

Accomplishments don't come from working a few minutes here and there. Accomplishments come from those periods in which we have the opportunity to engage in focused and purposeful work. In order to accomplish meaningful results, we must stay focused long enough to reach the area of greater results in the Results Curve™ before we switch to another task or allow ourselves to be interrupted. This is the Accomplishment Zone™.

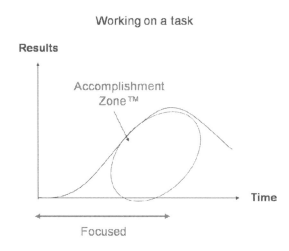

In the Accomplishment Zone™ we allow ourselves to experience deep thinking and creative problem solving. Here is where our brains can use their awesome power to discover hidden relationships between the parts as well as new and creative insights about the whole. This is where we can solve tough problems. This is where breakthroughs lie!

How Much Uninterrupted Time is Enough?

For most of our challenging work, it will be valuable for us to choose a consistent target time period that will get us into the Accomplishment Zone™ on a regular basis. In our workshops we've had participants indicate a preference for a 30 minute work period, while others want an entire hour. My suggestion is that we aim for an uninterrupted 40 minute period. My belief after working with thousands of people on productivity issues and challenges is that while 30 minutes is reasonable and achievable, after 30 minutes of focused work, the "engine" is now fully warmed

---

up and functioning optimally, so those extra 10 minutes are "pure" performance. Those 10 minutes are all in the high-potential area. We must grab them while we can.

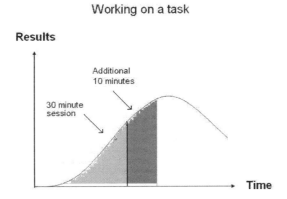

Working on a task

The Collaboration Zone™

When we create our Accomplishment Zone™, we block out interruptions great and small, including those that come from others in our work group. How do we make sure though that our own high performance time doesn't come at the expense of others?

After our highly focused session, in which we've "turned the world off" and focused on one important task, it will be time to switch gears and "turn the world on" again and engage into our collaborative activities. This is the Collaboration Zone™.

In the Collaboration Zone™, we handle e-mail messages, check voice messages, answer IM requests, and make ourselves available for virtual and in-person interactions. The Collaboration Zone™ can even include a social or private break. The collaborative session can be 10, 15, 30 minutes, or even longer, depending on how much collaborative work is necessary.

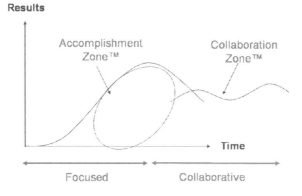

Working on a task

The Collaboration Zone™, shown in the graph above, is just as important as the Accomplishment Zone™. Together they satisfy the need to accomplish individual tasks and the need to connect and collaborate with the rest of the world. They help us resolve this ongoing conflict between focus and connectivity.

The collaborative session can also be energizing and enriching as we find out what went on out there while we were focusing on an individual task. It also brings a healthy dose of realism as we observe and collect data from an ever-changing environment. It helps us get back to our next focused session with a higher level of enthusiasm and better perspective. The collaborative session, together with the focused session, are the yin and yang of success in today's workplace.

The Killer Bs

What are the interruptions that keep us out of the Accomplishment Zone™? Our workshop participants are quick to point out e-mail, IM, phone calls, people dropping by, and our need or desire to take all sorts of breaks. But let's assume that we have all of these under control (which we will address soon and throughout this book). Let's say we've got a system for our e-mail and other digital interrupters. We've got a sign up so no one drops in on us. The phone is taking messages. So we're safe as far as these potential interruptions are concerned. Now are we going to be in the Accomplishment Zone™ without interruption for 40 minutes?

Well, not exactly. That is because none of the above mentioned interruptions capture the single and most noteworthy enemy of us successfully controlling our precious 40 minutes. There's one interrupter left, and it doesn't come from the outside. This interruption is our own wandering thoughts. The #1 killer of the Accomplishment Zone™ is us! Our own wandering thoughts are by far the primary cause for interrupting our current task and derailing us into new and often unrelated territories.

Thoughts are powerful. Thoughts can be valuable and relevant to the task at hand. We need those thoughts to do our work – to imagine, to evaluate, to think and create. But the way our minds naturally work means that our thoughts aren't always directed to the task at hand. When our thoughts help our work, we are controlling them. When our thoughts take us away from our work, they are controlling us.

Imagine me working on budget projections for the quarter. As I try to think about how much I should allow for online advertisement, my gaze drifts up as I contemplate what the right number might be. My gaze settles on the photo on my desk. Me in Paris. What a lovely trip that was last year. Except for the price of gas. I can remember that gas station where I stopped to fill up. I can see the numbers flashing past 90 euros. No question Hertz should be renting hybrids or electrics. I then start browsing the internet to see if anyone is renting hybrids in Europe.

I've gone from the photo lying on my desk, to browsing the Internet for the next 10 to 20 minutes. It is not inconceivable that while browsing the Internet, I notice that a new e-mail has arrived in my inbox. I hear the beep and take a look at the new e-mail message and start to reply to it. Meanwhile, I glance at the spam filter folder, and notice that there are number of new messages there. I abandon the e-mail message and start going through my spam filter. Another 10 or 20 minutes go by. Suddenly I realize that I am way off track, and ask myself the question "What the heck was I working on?"

Focusing on Task A

I call the work we are trying to accomplish Task A. Task A represents the work that is our most important work. It's what we want to do. It's what our team wants us to do, too. If we do all our Task As, we accomplish all of our life's desire. Accomplishment lies in racking up those Task As. Ideally, in the Accomplishment Zone™, we would focus on Task A and perform activities related to Task A until Task A is finished or until we've at least made significant progress on it.

In essence, our well-behaved mind would have thoughts related to Task A which are shown in the diagram below as Thoughts A1, A2, and A3.

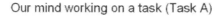

Our mind working on a task (Task A)

Promoting Killer B

Unfortunately, reality tends to be a little different from this ideal. Typically, soon after we start working on Task A, Thought B comes along. What in the world is Thought B doing here? Who knows, but it's here. What do we do when thought B comes along?

As shown below, more often than not, when Thought B comes along, we are likely to get kidnapped by it. We shift our line of thinking to Thought B while abandoning Task A. Thought B is a threat to continuing to work on our goal which is Task A. Thought B is dangerous. Thought B is in fact, a Killer B. Seriously — a kind of thought so bad we call it a "killer?" Yes. It's that bad.

Thought B pops up in our mind

When we give our attention to Thought B and begin to think about what it means, and begin to make associations for it, and begin to play with it, we let Thought B take over our consciousness. Until we can regain control of our senses, we have abandoned work on Thought A and Task A.

Capturing Killer B

What options do we have other than promoting Killer B? What would be a more constructive option? We could "capture" Killer B, so we can free our mind from it and return to it later if necessary.

Where do we capture Killer B? On the "Capture" page in a valuable tool I will introduce shortly: a paper journal. The primary purpose of the "Capture" page is to capture Killer Bs as quickly as possible and return to the task at hand.

Paper. How analog. Why not capture Killer B in electronic format? Why not file it where it belongs right away? Isn't this what the "touch once" theory has been promoting in the workplace for years?

The problem with capturing the errant thought in an electronic format is that it takes too much time. It pulls us away from Task A long enough to truly derail us. This would be the equivalent of reinforcing Killer B. If we truly believe that Task A is important, and we are serious about getting into the Accomplishment Zone™, we want to spend the least amount of time on getting Killer B out of the way. We live in a different time environment that requires different measures. We are no longer talking in terms of minutes but of seconds.

This means there is no time for opening or activating a desktop application, accessing the Web, using a stylus or touch screen, organizing, prioritizing, or philosophizing. There is only time to capture 3 to 5 key words, in 3 to 5 seconds, on the one and only Capture page, in the one and only paper journal, by the one and only *me*, in my own handwriting that no one else needs to understand. The Capture page in the paper journal is the path to the Accomplishment Zone™.

Ignoring Killer B

Are all thoughts worth capturing? Thankfully not. Otherwise, some of us would spend most of our time capturing the multitude of thoughts that keep popping up into our busy and creative minds.

If we determine that Killer B is just a random thought and is not worth capturing because its future value is insignificant, it makes more sense to ignore it and get back to task A as soon as possible, as illustrated below:

Turning Killer B into Useful B

It is possible that Killer B proves not to be a "killer" after all. It may be that Killer B has some value to add to Task A. This is actually the way our mind works sometimes. It unexpectedly brings an interesting thought that may not be directly related to Task A but that has some correlation to it and some applicable insights. Perhaps another approach to solving a problem that is key to Task A, or a relevant issue that we hadn't identified before. In this case, it is best to "integrate" the useful aspects of Killer B into Task A, and therefore turn Killer B into Useful B, as illustrated below:

Resisting Killer B

Sometimes, when we notice that we have been the victim of Killer B, and have been promoting Killer B or even actively contributing to its success at pulling us off Task A, we get into self-blame. The self-talk that we engage in can range from "I shouldn't be thinking about B right now" to the other extreme, which might be "I am a loser for thinking about B" or even "I will never get it right" and "I never get *anything* right," as our thinking grows increasingly irrational.

This is what we call "resisting" Killer B. Resisting Killer B is active—it's another form of promoting, and is just as harmful to our accomplishments. But resistance is a choice, and we can make another one. One way to do so is to reframe the resistance and reword the resisting thoughts. Instead of "I shouldn't be thinking about B," the alternative might be "I am glad that I noticed that I was thinking about B, and now that I did, I can get back to Task A." Reframing turns a problem into an opportunity.

How Do We Stay Focused?

Awareness alone is not enough to consistently keep us from running afoul of the thoughts that threaten our focus. We need more tangible and practical techniques to help us develop the ability to focus and cultivate "focus" as a habit.

First Technique: Using a timer

Not any timer – a countdown timer. Setting the countdown timer for 40 minutes (or whatever time period we choose) and then pushing the Start button has significant implications.

Just the fact that the timer is running seems to drastically heighten our awareness of time and allow us to quickly notice when we deviate from our task. It's as simple as that. It is fascinating that such a simple and easy tool can have such an impact on our focus, but it does. Buying a countdown timer may very well result in the biggest return on investment that we can ever achieve.

The Timer Creates Purpose

The timer helps us put a stake in the ground and declare that we have officially started the task at hand. Without such a clear signal it is easy to stay noncommittal, starting one task but then casually withdrawing from it to start another one. It is possible to keep testing task after task, escaping from the ones that are more difficult or less desirable, and sneaking into tasks that are easier (and, just as likely, less crucial) – I call this "task hopping!"

The timer puts an end to unproductive task hopping. It forces us to spend our time more purposefully on the task that we consciously select. This is a giant leap to become more purposeful. If you are thinking the timer is "just" another tool, and an expendable one at that, think again! The timer is revolutionary.

The Timer Creates Accountability

In addition to creating purpose, the timer also creates accountability. Now that the timer has started, in 40 minutes we are going to know clearly if we accomplished what we intended. The timer also helps us estimate time better in the future. Knowing how long it takes to accomplish any given project in such a time-crunched era is a rare and highly desirable skill.

The timer prompts us to move things forward

During the focused session, the timer improves the quality and efficiency of our work. It prompts us to face the issues, make decisions, and move things along as opposed to dwelling on issues and staying indefinitely in analysis/paralysis mode. In other words, the timer accelerates our pace and helps us equal or even beat the speed at which things are happening around us. What a competitive advantage that can be!

The timer as a stress relief mechanism

The timer signifies that we have given ourselves permission to be where we are for the time period we have chosen. Now we can more easily give up the guilt or anxiety that we would otherwise experience for not being somewhere else and not handling all the other things that need to be handled. With the timer, we are able to put everything else on hold because we have more "officially" chosen a path, and most importantly a path based on purpose instead of a reactive one. The timer is the official seal of approval for our purposeful choice.

With the timer and the 40 minute sessions, instead of feeling guilty and anxious, we feel challenged to complete our carefully selected mission. Instead of taking on "life" and feeling overwhelmed and trapped, now we are taking on 40 minutes, and feeling hopeful. We are fully engaged and facing the issues for 40 minutes with a visible and bright light shining at the end of tunnel. What a relief!

The happy sound of accomplishment

The happy sound of accomplishment is only 40 minutes away, and when it is heard, we are likely to experience a range of thoughts and feelings, the most prevalent of which is likely to be satisfaction.

Stopping is critical at this juncture. Even a brief moment of acknowledgement goes a long way. This can take any form that is appropriate for the context. Sometimes a few minutes of letting our mind freely wander and allowing thoughts and feelings to surface can do the job. Sometimes this may require a more significant break and potentially some physical movement that gets us re-energized.

Which timer works best?

Any timer will do, but not all timers are equal. Timers that are software applications that can run on our computers are easy to find and many of them are free. However they tend to hide behind other applications on our busy computer desktops and therefore their role as a persistent reminder of time tends to diminish. Also, in a world of everything-electronic and everything-virtual, a physical item is likely to stand out and be noticed. In addition, an object that we can manipulate with our hands is likely to awaken and evoke motor skills that will add to the quality of our overall experience. All these factors considered, a physical countdown timer is best.

Second Technique: Micro-Planning™ each 40 minute session

Creating a brief outline at the beginning of each 40 minute session listing key steps that we need to get done in order to complete the selected task can make the session as successful as it can be, as illustrated in the example below:

Task	Update projections
Micro-Plan™	Download the latest spreadsheet
	Review the most recent guidelines
	Update the formulas accordingly
	Regenerate PivotTables and graphs
	Upload updated version
	Schedule meeting to review with team

Ideally the Micro-Plan™ is handwritten in just a minute or two in the Notes section in the paper journal that we will introduce in the next chapter.

Just like the timer, which appears to be a simple and perhaps expendable tool on the surface, Micro-Planning™ is a powerful technique that can help us stay focused, and if and when we have to deviate to take care of urgent issues, the Micro-Plan™ helps us restart our task with the minimum amount of effort and the fastest recovery time.

As we get deeper into our task, the Micro-Plan™ can continue to evolve and serve as the short-term parking lot for new potential steps or related ideas that would otherwise derail us from the current steps. Our mind stays fully available for the core issues we are processing now. The Micro-Plan™ and the journal become our thinking pad and the extension of, and support system for, our short term memory, which tends to be challenged as information continues to relentlessly invade our mind space.

Micro-Planning™ and the timer work together to help achieve focus, purpose, and results that will add up to meaningful accomplishments.

Third Technique: Turning Off External Interruptions

It sounds simple, and it would be if all external interruptions were within our control. Wishful thinking!

Indeed, we can turn off the e-mail beep, forward the phone to voice mail, and indicate that we are busy or "away" in our Instant Messaging status, which we should do during our focus sessions. But it is much more difficult to switch off the people who stop by, the noise or conversations around our work area, and most importantly the urgent and critical requests that come from bosses, colleagues, customers, family and friends, not to mention the blame and guilt that come from not being available to handle all of the above promptly.

The answer to these external challenges is certainly not simple but it is an area where we have more influence than we tend to believe. To better manage these group-inflicted interruptions, it is imperative to a) find an agreed upon way in which we communicate to our team that we are focused (whether it is putting up a sign in our work area, or setting our IM status appropriately), and b) find an agreed upon way in which our team can escalate critical issues to us when such issues come up (whether it is cell phone, pager, or a special keyword in IM):

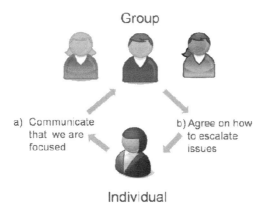

The answer also lies in negotiating effectively with the world to help align goals and priorities and to optimize how responsibilities and tasks are divided and distributed. Using collaboration technologies is essential in this effort and so is developing best practices around these technologies so they support us in this effort instead of hindering us.

In a way, this whole book is dedicated to acquiring the skills, and learning the methodology, that are essential for smart negotiating and for using technology effectively. To negotiate successfully, we need to have clarity, we need to have a purpose, and we need to have data, among other things. It is one thing to step into our boss's office and say, "I am overwhelmed and cannot get my work done." It is quite something else to show our boss a list of the competing priorities broken down into tasks and arranged in a timeline, with some initial thoughts on potential solutions that can serve as a catalyst for negotiation and for creative problem-solving (this is what the Immediate Priorities Matrix™ will introduce in a later chapter).

In Summary

Let us move away from feeling hectic and head towards feeling calm. Let us move away from feeling overwhelmed and head towards feeling fulfilled. Let us move away from mediocrity and head towards accomplishment. The Accomplishment Zone™ leads to a life of accomplishments, 40 minutes at a time. It is compelling. It is satisfying. It is yours, now.

Exercise 1: Managing Interruptions

List the main sources of interruptions in your work environment. Reflect on how much influence you have on each source, and what actions can you take to help minimize it.

Table 1: Managing Interruptions

Source	How much influence do I have over it?	What action will I take to eliminate it or minimize it so I can stay focused and reach the Accomplishment Zone™?

Exercise 2: Creating agreements

Reflect on ways in which you and your team can collaborate more effectively. Educate your team about the Results Curve™, Accomplishment Zone™, and Collaboration Zone™, and agree with them on how you want to communicate to each other when you are focused, and how you escalate issues when such issues come up.

Table 2: Creating agreements

Ideas for how to notify my group that I am focused	Ideas for defining what a critical issues is (the criteria that make an issue critical)	Ideas for how to escalate critical issues

Exercise 3: Micro-Planning™

Identify an important task that you would like to accomplish soon. Block time on your calendar to focus on this task (at least 40 minutes). At the beginning of this focused session, time yourself, and spend a few minutes putting together the Micro-Plan™ using the table below:

Table 3: Micro-Planning™

Steps	Comment/Description

Action Plan

Identify the action items that you would like to take as a result of what was covered in this chapter. Indicate the timeframe in which you plan on taking these actions. Then report on the actual date in which you implemented them and a brief note about the results.

Table 4: Action Plan

Practice/Technique	I will start implementing this on (date?)	Actual start date	Actual end date	Comment/Results
Working in focused sessions (40 minute, or your desired length)				
Using a timer				
Using Micro-Planning™				
Educating my team				
Agree with my team on how we communicate to each other when we are focused				
Agree with my team on defining what makes an issue critical				
Agree with my team on how to escalate issues				
Add your own item:				
Add your own item:				
Add your own item:				

Chapter 2: Meet Your New (Non-Digital) Assistant—simplify your life with the journal

Don't let the simplicity of the journal and how we are going to use it initially deceive you. Our workshop graduates incorporate the journal into their mix of tools and adapt it to fit their unique situation. It is fascinating to see what they have done with their journals.

If you're thinking "but I do everything electronically", you will soon discover the journal perfectly supplements the electronic world and plays an important role in helping us gain depth and perspective. The majority of this book is dedicated to electronic tools. But for now, hold on tight, and discover the journal.

Today's Page

If you haven't yet gotten your hands on a journal, this is the time to do so. Open your journal to a blank page, write down today's date, and then below it, write down a brief outline of what you intend to accomplish today, as shown below (for now, and for the purpose of practicing, let us have one accomplishment, which is "Learn how to use the journal"):

The Capture Page

On the next page, write the heading: Capture. This page is for to-do items and ideas that you encounter throughout the day, things you don't want to handle immediately but will instead capture and handle at a more convenient time.

The Notes Page

And now flip to a new page and write down: Notes. This page is for meeting notes, phone conversion notes, thinking and strategizing notes.

When you're taking notes, and you happen to write down an item that you would like to act upon or follow-up on later, you may want to draw a little checkbox next to the item. Later when you review this page, the checkbox serves as a visual reminder for the action or follow-up. Then when you take the appropriate action or transfer the item to the to-do list or calendar, you can check it off.

Notes

Meeting with product team:
- Updated timeline
- Need a additional developer
☑ *Check with Dawn on John's availablity next week*

When writing notes, I recommend writing clearly and succinctly. It is more about capturing the essence rather than every single detail. It is about quality, not quantity. If you are a heavy note taker, I invite you to take fewer notes and stay connected with what is going on around you instead of being consumed by note taking. If you normally don't take any notes, and find yourself forgetting or missing certain parts of the conversation or important follow-up action items, you may want to start taking notes, capturing the key points and action items.

Writing legibly is also important, not only so that we will be able to read it more easily later, but it helps us slow down a bit and really notice what is going on around us. It enables us to write more thoughtfully, to write only what is important, and it sends the subconscious message to us and the people around us, that what we are writing is important.

One question that comes up sometimes in the workshop is why take notes on the journal when we can just use a laptop, or a PDA, or a smartphone? It is very tempting to do so, and it may be appropriate in some situations, such as if you are the designated minutes taker in a group meeting, or in some cultures where it is accepted and almost expected, such as Google. Otherwise, taking notes on a laptop or a PDA or a smartphone is likely to take your attention away from the more important non-verbal communication. You are likely to miss noticing body language where real communication takes place. It is also likely to be distracting to the other party as they miss your eye contact and your ongoing non-verbal feedback. In a way, it may cut short the benefits of the conversation.

Taking notes in the journal is less intrusive, usually much quieter, and much faster. You can jot down a few words in seconds, while your posture stays connected and engaged. You can resume eye contact, and not miss a beat of what is going on. This is more than note taking. This is preserving human connection and relationship building.

Finally, one practical side to the journal is that it can be with you at all times, it takes no time to get it out and open it, and it never runs out of battery.

Exercise: What are you hoping to accomplish?

Let us put the notes page to use right away. Take a minute to jot down the reasons why you are reading this book. In other words, what are the main challenges you face in getting organized, managing your to-do lists, managing your time, and reaching your goals? Maybe even list the areas in which you are experiencing stress.

I would like to remind you here about the technique that I introduced in the previous chapter: using a timer to focus yourself when working on certain tasks. Timing ourselves helps us stay focused on the issue at hand instead of letting our mind wander to unwanted territories. Timing ourselves also prompts us to move forward and make decisions instead of staying in analysis mode longer than necessary. Overall, it helps us apply our energy and sustain our attention to desired places. Start practicing the timing techniques now and give yourself one minute to finish the above exercise.

When we conduct this exercise in our workshop, we get a variety of answers including getting organized, feeling more in control, and managing competing priorities. We also get more specific answers relating to issues that participants are dealing with at the time, such as handling a difficult project task or issue, dealing with a difficult situation or a difficult person, or lacking motivation in a certain area.

Whatever you wrote down in your journal, it is likely that over the course of this book, you will find insights, concepts, and techniques that will help you tremendously in these areas, maybe even create a breakthrough. For now, we are going to put this to the side, and refer to it later in the book, especially when we formulate the action plan towards the end. Now you are ready to proceed with the next chapter, moving into yet another paper related topic – organizing the desk.

Action Plan

Identify the action items that you would like to take as a result of what was covered in this chapter. Indicate the timeframe in which you plan on taking these actions. Then report on the actual date in which you implemented them and a brief note about the results.

Table 1: Action Plan

Practice/Technique	I will start implementing this on (date?)	Actual start date	Actual end date	Comment/Results
Getting a journal				
Starting to use the journal on a daily basis				
Starting a new page for each day and listing what I intend to accomplish				
Starting the Capture Page for capturing items that you want to deal with later				
Starting the Notes page for notes, and using checkboxes to identify items that require action or follow-up				
Add your own item:				
Add your own item:				
Add your own item:				

Chapter 3: Mastering the Personal Zone—get paperwork under control

In this chapter we will cover some simple yet very powerful concepts that can help you organize your desk and are also applicable to the electronic world and to organization in general. So even if your desk is organized, or you don't deal much with papers, you will find the material covered in this chapter quite helpful and insightful.

Today's Page

Before we get started with the desk, let us first turn to a new page in the journal – a new day, a new page. Open your journal to a new page, and write down today's date, and then right below it, write down a brief outline of what you intend to accomplish today, as shown below:

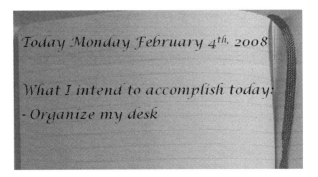

Then start the Capture page. As we explained in the journal chapter, use this page to jot down to-do items and ideas you encounter throughout the day that you don't want to handle immediately but rather capture and handle at a time when it is more convenient.

And finally, start the Notes page, where you capture meetings notes, phone conversation notes, thinking and strategizing notes.

As you read through this chapter, you can use the notes page to jot down key concepts we are covering and thoughts you have about the topic. Make use of the journal. This is your workspace.

Organizing the desk

Organizing the desk involves the demonstration of three techniques, one relating to loose papers and piles that we tend to have on and around our desk area, the second relating to reference material that may be scattered in our work area and that we refer to often, and the third relating to the inflow of papers and how we process them when they arrive to our workspace.

First Technique: The Work-In-Progress Unit

Why do we normally have scattered papers and piles of papers on and around our desk area?

Figure 1: Scattered papers on our desk

One reason is that we start to work on an item, but we get interrupted and move to another item. We leave the first item on our desk as a reminder, and with the hope that we will get back to it sooner than later. This happens again and again, and eventually our desk becomes full of these papers which we will refer to as work-in-progress papers.

To organize the work in progress papers, we are going to use a filing unit with hanging folders. This can be a filing drawer underneath the desk area or in a close by filing cabinet that is convenient. It can even be a portable filing unit. We will refer to this unit as the Work-In-Progress Unit.

Figure 2: Sample Work-In-Progress Unit

We will now gather the work-in-progress papers, not in any particular order – picking up each paper or set of papers that belong to the same issue or project, putting them in a paper folder, labeling it quickly by hand, and putting it in the Work-In-Progress Unit.

Figure 3: Related papers in a folder in the Work-In-Progress Unit

Then we take the next set of papers that relate to the next issue or project, and put them in yet another paper folder, hand label it quickly, and put it behind the previous folder in the Work-In-Progress Unit. Note that at this point, we are not concerned about ordering or prioritizing them.

Figure 4: Continuing the process one folder after another

We continue with the above process until all the loose papers are tucked in folders in the Work-In-Progress Unit. The benefit to this task is that we have transformed the scattered papers on our desk, which were difficult to work with, into small packets of information that are easy to go through to find desired information. However the more significant benefits of the Work-In-Progress Unit will become apparent now as we get into the details of how it is used on a daily basis.

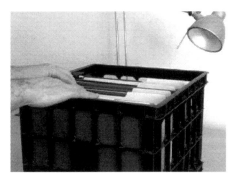

Figure 5: Scattered papers are now all in the Work-In-Progress Unit

The Work-In-Progress Unit in action

Now that we have our work-in-progress papers in the Work-In-Progress Unit, let's examine how we are going to use them on an on-going basis and reap the benefits.

Let us say I start working on a certain issue or project, and I realize that I need the related papers in the Work-In-Progress Unit. Therefore I go through the Work-In-Progress Unit, and find the necessary folder. Then I proceed with my work on this issue or project, making use of the papers in this folder as necessary. Now, let's say I am done with what I need to do for now, however, I am still not completely finished with this issue or project, and I am likely to refer to this folder again when I resume my work later.

What do I do with the folder for the time being? Obviously I would put it back in the Work-In-Progress Unit (after all, this folder still represents work that is in progress). The important question however is: "Where exactly do I put the folder in the Work-In-Progress Unit"? Do I put it in the same location where I got it from? That would be difficult to figure out knowing that the unit is not ordered alphabetically or in any predetermined sort order.

This brings us to the first concept I would like to cover relating to organizing the desk, which will also apply to the electronic world later: the most recently used goes on top. According to this concept, when I put the folder back in the Work-In-Progress Unit, I put it back in front of all the other folders—the most recently used goes on top.

Figure 6: The most recently used folder goes in front

Let's take another example. In this case, I get a phone call related to an issue or project whose papers are also in a folder in the Work-In-Progress Unit. I quickly go through my work-in-progress folders, find the relevant folder, and pull it out. I then go through the papers within this folder and find the exact paper that I need for this conversation.

When I am done with my phone call, where should I put this paper?

The same concept applies. I put this paper on top within the folder, and then I put the folder back in the front of the Work-In-Progress Unit. So the "most recently used goes on top" concept applies even within each of the work-in-progress folders.

Figure 7: The most recently used goes on top even within the folder

As a result of the above, what will happen over time is that the folders that are in use continue to gravitate towards the front while the unused ones slowly but surely gravitate towards the back. In a few weeks or months, depending on your work cycle, you could take out a bunch of folders from the back, review each folder and identify whether the related issue or project is now finished. If finished, then the folder can be transferred to the filing cabinet, or otherwise recycled or shredded. If it is not finished, the folder is placed back in the Work-In-Progress Unit.

Out of sight out of mind?

But we are taking these papers out of sight, and isn't "out of sight is out of mind"? This is what some workshop participants say when we first talk about the Work-In-Progress Unit.

The out of sight out of mind concept is a misleading one as most participants end up realizing. First of all, when these papers are scattered on our desk, or in piles around our desk, they are no longer in sight. They are hiding each other and are often very difficult to go through. Second, even if these papers are well organized on our desk and not hiding each other, after a day or two, we get used to having them in sight, and we start to think of them as being part of the environment. They no longer serve as reminders. Therefore "in sight" does not necessarily mean "in mind."

"Out of sight out of mind" may work well if you have a few items to deal with, enough desk space to nicely spread them out, and if you are diligent at reviewing them and handling them in a timely manner. But once you have more than just a few items, without the luxury of a large desk space, and with the competing priorities and conflicting demands of today's information overload, the Work-In-Progress Unit will serve you better. When it comes to time sensitive items in the Work-In-Progress Unit, we recommend including specific reminders on the calendar or to-do list, which are discussed in upcoming chapters. Today's information overload requires a more structured and robust approach when it comes to tracking time sensitive items.

Second Technique: The Quick Reference Unit

The second technique relates to reference material that may be currently scattered in our work area. We are talking about information that doesn't change often and that doesn't require action. Examples are: Telephone lists, organizational charts, event schedules, product codes, just to mention a few. To help organize such reference material, I will introduce the Quick Reference Unit. This unit can be a vertical folder unit as shown below or a drawer in a filing cabinet that is easy to get to.

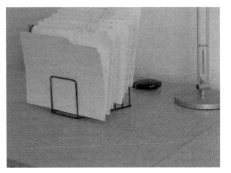

Figure 8: The Quick Reference Unit

Without having the Quick Reference Unit, this information would be scattered across our desk, pinned on our walls, or stored in electronic documents, just to mention a few places. The Quick Reference Unit consolidates this information in one place that is easy to reach.

Other examples of Quick Reference material would be project lists, maps and directions, and even articles or reading material that we would like to read when time allows. Next time we are going on a train ride or plane ride, we can grab the appropriate folders and slide them in our briefcase or bag.

Third Technique: The Inbox, Outbox, and Maybe Later Box

The third technique relates to the inbox, outbox, and Maybe Later Box shown below:

Figure 9: Inbox, outbox, Maybe Later Box

The inbox holds incoming papers that we haven't looked at yet, and that we still need to sort through. The outbox holds outgoing papers such as outgoing mail or documents that need to be distributed or handed over to others. If you don't deal with a lot of paper, you may not need a physical inbox and outbox. If this is the case, incoming and outgoing papers could just lie on your desk until they are handled. This may be okay if you handle these papers in a timely manner and if you don't have lots of them. Otherwise introducing the inbox and outbox in your work area may be helpful. Either way, it is the Maybe Later Box that is the most important here, and the focus of our discussion.

But what is the Maybe Later Box? The Maybe Later Box relates to creating space for papers that a) don't require further action (and therefore don't belong to our Work-In-Progress Unit), b) are not important enough to be filed in our filing cabinet (we don't want to spend time filing them and we don't want them to occupy precious filing space), but c) we are not yet willing to let go of them, thinking that it is conceivable that they may be of use in the future.

If we don't have a Maybe Later Box, these papers would take over our desk space, pile up around our desk area, and end up being the "noise" that hides the important papers and distracts us from what is relevant. The Maybe Later Box consolidates these papers in one place, keeps them out of our way, while having them still available for future reference if/when the need arises.

Occasionally you may find yourself referring to the Maybe Later Box, searching for a product brochure or vacation destination that you received a few weeks or months ago. It should be easy to find this paper by going through the Maybe Later Box where information is stored in reverse chronological order—with the most recent on top. When you find the desired paper, you can refer to it, take the necessary action and move it to the appropriate place. Then once or twice a year, you can take the papers that are older than three or six months and get rid of them.

Handling papers that come our way

Now that we have demonstrated the techniques, here is the summary diagram:

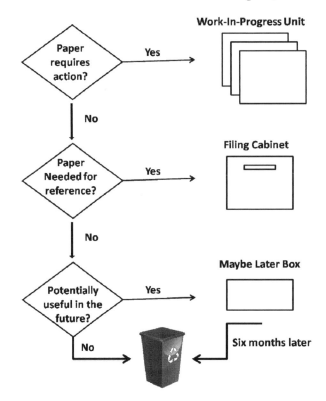

The concepts behind the techniques

First Concept: The most recently used goes on top

We already highlighted the first of three concepts that are behind the techniques we described earlier. The first concept was "the most recently used goes on top". This applies to the Work-In-Progress Unit and within each work-in-progress folder. We also used it in the Maybe Later Box. Let us now introduce and discuss the other two concepts.

Second Concept: Having designated holding areas

Each of the areas we discussed is actually a designated holding area. This includes the Work-In-Progress Unit, the Quick Reference Unit, the inbox, the outbox, the Maybe Later Box, and the to-be filed box if you choose to have one. What makes these areas designated holding areas is not only that they are designated physical

---

spaces, but also that we have designated how we are going to use them and specifically which papers belong to which area. If we don't "have designated holding areas", out whole work area become one big designated holding area that is difficult to manage.

Third Concept: Creating distance

This implies distancing ourselves from information before we get too busy prematurely organizing it, prioritizing it, and acting on it. This is exactly what the Work-In-Progress Unit is about. This is also what the Maybe Later Box is about. These designated holding areas help us semi-organize information quickly and easily. They give us a chance to absorb what is going on and gain more experience with the information before we get too invested in it. In other words, they create necessary "distance".

In a world where information is coming at us in abundance at high speed, we need this "distance" to slow things down a bit. We need the "designated holding areas" to quickly and easily semi-organize information so it doesn't get out of control. We need to apply the "most recently used on top" rule to keep the most relevant information in front of us. The end result is that a) the noise is out of the way and the core information is easily accessible, b) we have more time to deal with the core issues instead of prematurely organizing, and c) most important we have better clarity and better perspective.

Implement as you please

Throughout this chapter, and the rest of the book, we present concepts and demonstrate specific techniques to show you how these concepts can be applied in your daily work life. Some participants implement the techniques exactly as demonstrated, while others tailor them, expand on them, or even re-invent them to fit their own needs and unique situations. We encourage you to experiment and adapt the techniques as you wish. The sky is the limit.

The Accomplishing-more-with-less methodology, as you may have noticed already, is intended to be modular and flexible. It is not an "all or nothing" approach. There is plenty of room for you to customize. You can pick and choose the elements you need and adapt them to your environment. Then add additional ones later when the need arises.

The ultimate goal of the Accomplishing-more-with-less methodology is to give you the foundation and the guidance to get started on this journey of accomplishment and self-fulfillment. How exactly you go about implementing it is all up to you!

Action Plan

Identify the action items that you would like to use as a result of what was covered in this chapter. Indicate the timeframe in which you plan on taking these actions. Then report on the actual date in which you implemented them and a brief note about the results.

Table 1: Action Plan

Practice/Technique	I will start implementing this on (date?)	Actual start date	Actual end date	Comment/Results
Designating space for the work-in-progress folders				
Designating space for quick-reference material				
Designating space for the maybe-later papers and material				
Having supplies ready (folders, pencils, etc.)				
Clearing the desk by moving papers to work-in-progress				
Add your own item:				
Add your own item:				
Add your own item:				

Chapter 4: E-mail Subdued—organize your e-mail inbox in no time

E-mail has become the obsession and addiction of today's digital age. In this chapter we will examine techniques to help us recover and regain control of our time and our priorities instead of being e-mail driven, and continuously pulled into different random directions (instead of staying focused and reaching the Accomplishment Zone™).

Today's pages

Before we get started with e-mail, let us turn to a new page in the journal – a new day, a new page. Write down today's date, and then below it, write down a brief outline of what we intend to accomplish today, as shown below:

Today Tuesday February 5th, 2008

What I intend to accomplish today:
- Organize e-mail

Start the Capture Page, and again use this page to jot down to-do items and ideas that you encounter throughout the day, that you don't want to handle immediately, but rather capture and handle at a time when it is more convenient.

Capture Page

And finally, start the Notes Page, where you capture meetings notes, phone conversion notes, thinking and strategizing notes.

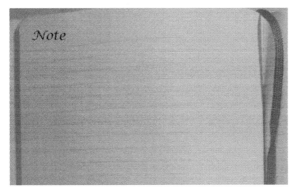

Customizing your email toolbar

We are going to demonstrate the tips and techniques in Outlook 2003. However as you will see, the key concepts are applicable in any e-mail application. Even if you are not using Outlook, go through this session, and note key concepts, and then apply them to your own e-mail application. For those using later versions of Outlook (such as 2007 or 2010), you can refer to Appendix A for additional information and coupons relating to our online live workshops that cover these versions.

Before we get to the inbox, let us first customize the toolbar and add a few helpful commands to it. From the Tools menu, select Customize to open the Customize window as shown below. Select the Commands tab, and from the categories list on the left, select Action. In the Commands list on the right side, scroll down until you get to the flags. Drag the red flag, the blue flag, the yellow flag, and the Add Reminder commands to the toolbar. You have to drag each of these commands individually to the toolbar.

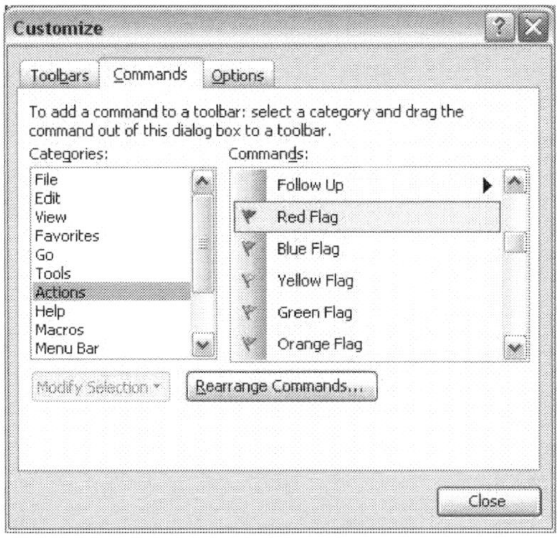

Figure 10: Customize Window

When you are done, close the Customize window, and your toolbar should look similar to this:

Figure 11: The toolbar with the new commands

The reason we added these commands to the toolbar is mainly convenience. As we will see soon, I will use these commands quite often, and instead of going through several layers of menus and mouse clicks to use them, I can now access them with one click. Let's put them to use.

Processing the inbox

I'm going to go through my inbox (from top to bottom) and examine each message and decide what to do about it.

When I encounter a message that can be responded to quickly and easily, I respond to it and get it out of the way. This involves moving it immediately out of the inbox. We have a lot more to say about this, but we will save it until later in this chapter when we address the question of filing messages.

When I encounter a message that I cannot handle right away, I quickly decide when I am going to handle it, and then flag it appropriately. For instance, let us consider the message from Delora which is shown below, and let us assume that this is a message that I cannot handle right way, but that I would like to handle later today. Therefore I select the message, and then click on the red flag button which I just placed on the toolbar. This clearly identifies this message as needing my attention sometime today.

Figure 12: Message with red flag

Let us consider the second message in my inbox which is from Chris and which I am not going to handle right away but I would like to get to it later today. First I flag it with a red flag. Second, I click on the Add Reminder button on the toolbar and setup the appropriate reminder as shown below. When the time comes, the reminder window opens up and displays the message.

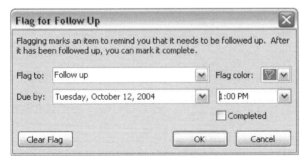

Figure 4: Adding a reminder to a message

And now my inbox looks like this:

Figure 5: Messages with red flags

Let us now proceed to the third message also from Chris. This is a message that I will not handle right now, and that doesn't need to be handled today. I click on the blue flag button on the toolbar to assign it the blue flag. I am using the blue flag to indicate that this message still requires a reply or an action of some sort, but that it can wait until tomorrow or the next few days.

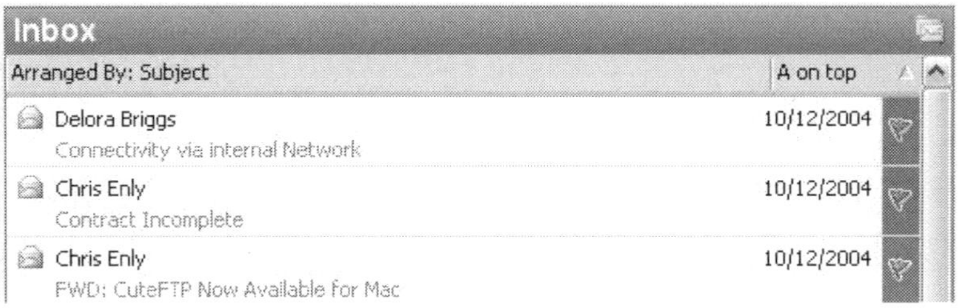

Figure 6: Message with blue flag

Let us now continue with the message from Crystal which relates to an issue that I would like to delegate to one of my team members. I forward a copy of the message to the intended team member adding my comments as necessary. What should I do then with the original message in my inbox?

If I am not interested in following-up on this issue, I can simply file the original message away. However, if I am interested in keeping an eye on this issue, and making sure that it has been closed, I might choose to assign to it a yellow flag. I select the message and click the yellow flag button on the toolbar.

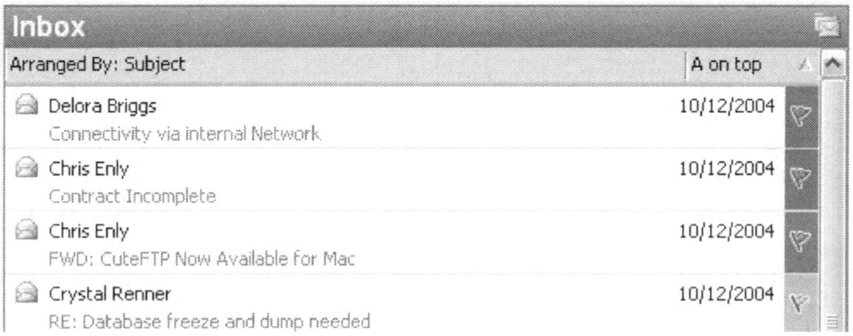

Figure 7: Messages with yellow flag

Please note that I can also assign reminders to messages with blue and yellow flags, just as I did earlier with the message with a red flag. For instance this last

---

message that I delegated to one of my team members may be time sensitive so I may click on Add Reminder, and assign the appropriate due date.

Reviewing flagged messages

Wouldn't be nice to be able to see all these flagged messages all in one place and nicely organized and grouped by the flag color? This would obviously make it easy and efficient to review them and act on them in a timely manner.

If you click on the For Follow-Up search folder in the left navigation pane in Outlook 2003, you will get a view of exactly that: The flagged messages nicely organized and grouped by flag color.

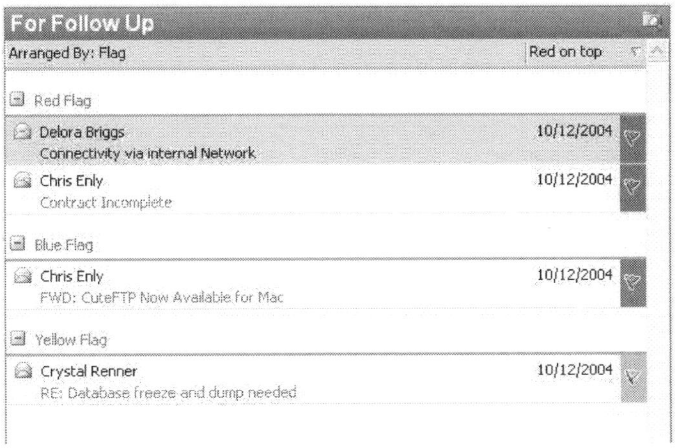

Figure 8: The For Follow-Up search folder

So what would you call this view? What descriptive name would you give it? Some participants like to call it "the e-mail to-do list" and rightfully so because it shows us clearly which e-mails need to be done and when.

Customizing the Inbox

Now I have the flagged messages nicely organized in the For Follow-up search folder but they are also visible in the inbox. Do I still need to see them in the inbox?

I have already decided the timeframe by which I will handle them. I have them nicely organized in the For Follow-Up search folder, and can periodically go back there to work on them, so I don't really need to have them visible in the inbox.

Keeping them visible in the inbox would be distracting. They would clutter the inbox and hide new and potentially more urgent messages. In addition, I am likely to go through the same thinking process I went through earlier, and arrive to the same conclusion I arrived at earlier, which is to handle them later.

To hide these messages from the inbox, I would like to customize the inbox view by right-mouse clicking on any column in the inbox, and from the popup menu that gets displayed, selecting the Customize Current View item. When the Customize View window is displayed, I click on the Filter button. This opens up the Filter window, in which I select the Advanced tab, and set the filter as shown below:

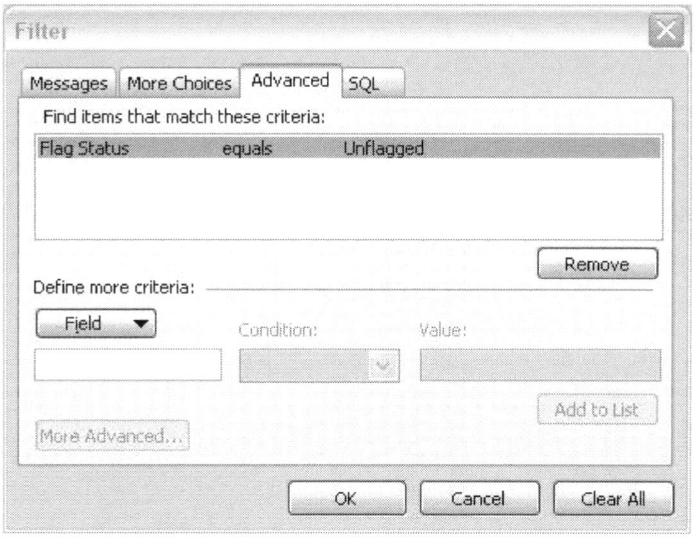

Figure 9: Adding a filter

Once I click OK, the flagged messages will disappear from the inbox, and will only be visible in the For Follow-Up search folder. As a result, my work in email is now clearly divided into two kinds of activities. The first consists of reviewing my inbox and handling urgent messages right away, as well as the easy ones, while flagging the other messages for later. The second consists of reviewing the For Follow-Up search folder and handling these outstanding messages in a timely manner.

What we haven't discussed yet at this point is the issue of when and how often we check the inbox, and when and how often do we work on the messages in the For

Follow-up Folder. These questions and decisions are at the heart of effective e-mail management, and we will discuss them in detail in the following two chapters as well as later when we get to the chapter about interruptions. For now, we are only building the foundation, piece by piece, and we will continue to do so in the remainder of this chapter.

Out of sight out of mind?

We are taking these e-mails out of sight when we flag them and they are no longer visible in the inbox – are we back to the adage out of sight out of mind? We discussed this objection earlier when we organized the Desk. Just as we indicated earlier, the out of sight out of mind belief is misleading. When all these messages are visible in the inbox, they are not exactly in sight, because you normally have to scroll down several pages to find them. The For Follow-Up search folder is only one click away. In addition, the messages in the For Follow-Up search folder are nicely organized and grouped by flag color, which makes them easy to review and process. Maybe it is time we put this "out of sight out of mind" belief out of mind once for all.

Filing Messages

When we discussed the inbox earlier, we indicated that once we handle a message, by taking the necessary action and replying to it, we move it immediately out of the inbox. We don't want finished messages to stay in the inbox and clutter it or hide new and important messages. Our job is not done until the message that we replied to is moved out of the inbox.

Now let us elaborate on this issue and examine how we can efficiently file these finished messages. By the way, our discussion does not apply to flagged messages. Flagged messages are not going to be filed for now. Once they are flagged they are no longer visible in the inbox. They are only visible in the For Follow-Up search folder. When we go back to them, and take the necessary action, then we will file them following the same concepts discussed here.

The 80/20 Rule

Before we discuss filing finished messages, there is an important concept that we need to cover first, and that is the 80/20 rule. Have you come across this rule?

If you work in sales, you may have heard that 80% of the revenues come from 20% of the customers. If you deal with technical support, you may have heard that 80% of the support issues come from 20% of the users. And there are many more examples. The one that I am interested in says: 80% of our results come from 20% of our effort. Yes, 80% of our results come from 20% of our effort.

80/20 Rule

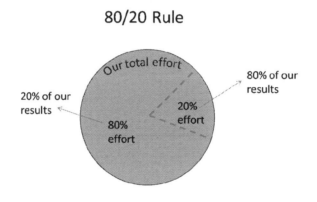

Figure 10: The 80/20 Rule

If you are surprised or think this is an exaggeration, do a little experiment. Keep a log of every task you engage in on a daily basis for several days. Then review the log and try to map it to the results that you are trying to accomplish. You are likely to be convinced. At any rate, the exact percentages are not the issue here. The main point is this: Most of what we accomplish comes from certain focused activities that we do and do well.

The 80/20 rule has many important implications. If we become more aware of this reality and apply strategic thinking to find out which of our activities creates most of our results, we can then do more of these activities and abandon other fruitless activities. If we increase the 20% to 30%, what do you think the total increase in our results will be?

80/20 Rule

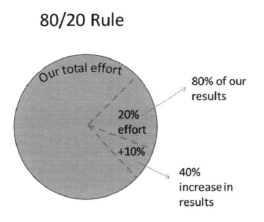

Figure 11: Increasing results

In fact, it would be about a 40% increase. This is a simple mathematical equation: 20% produces 80% of our results, so how much would 30% produce? It would produce 120% which is an extra 40%. So yes, a 10% increase in our core activities, would produce a 40% increase in the results. In other words, getting more accomplished is not about working harder and getting more done, it is about thinking strategically, and applying our time and resources in the most promising places.

The 80/20 Rule Applied to E-mail

So now let us apply this rule to e-mail. If 20% of our activities are likely to generate most of our results, we can extrapolate this to e-mail, and say that it is 20% of our e-mails that are generating most of our e-mail results. These are the core e-mails that relate to our core activities. The remaining 80% are likely to be more tactical and less important e-mails that don't have a significant impact on results.

Back to the topic of filing e-mails, once I reply to a message, where should I file it?

If this message belongs to the 20% group of e-mail messages, I suggest filing it in the appropriate folder. For this to work well, we would need to have a well-designed filing structure that reflects a) our key business drivers, b) our key audiences, and c) our key subject matters. We will go through this in detail in a few chapters. Here is a sample structure for a project manager at a technology company:

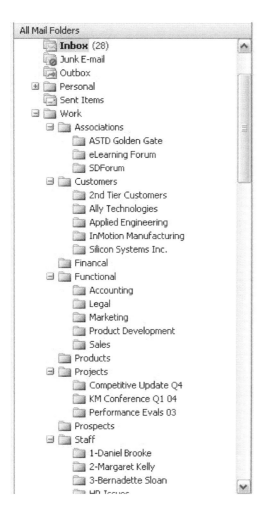

Figure 12: Sample e-mail filing structure

If this message happens to belong to the 80% group of e-mail messages which don't have much impact on results, we don't want to spend the time and energy filing it in folders. Filing can take significant time and energy. Instead, we want to create one catch-all folder where we file all such messages.

Some participants ask why don't we just delete such messages when we are done with them? There is nothing wrong with deleting these messages. There are a few issues to consider though. First, you want to be informed about the retention and deletion policy of your organization to make sure you are conforming to it. This is recommended not only for deleting e-mails, but for managing other electronic and paper documents as well. Second, it is possible that some e-mails that appear now to be tactical and not too important, may become suddenly important in the future when certain related issues come up. So keeping them for some time before deleting them may be a good idea. Third, deleting can sometimes take up time. It is not the deleting itself, but the decision process that we might go through. If you find yourself wondering whether you should delete the message or not, and questioning or hesitating, it is best to cut this short and just file the message in the catch-all folder.

Overall moving an e-mail message to the catch-all folder is quick, easy, and efficient, and a safe bet.

Did you give up on filing e-mail messages all together?

Several users I talked to have given up on filing e-mail messages all together because it became difficult if not impossible to keep up with the volume of e-mail and not to mention keep up with the extra time it would require to file it. So they resorted to keeping all e-mail messages in the inbox, including finished messages, and then archiving the inbox from time to time or when necessary.

Why not follow their approach? Why not just keep the e-mail in the inbox or file it all in the catch all folder? After all, this is the Google way. If you have used Gmail, you are pretty familiar with it. Instead of filing e-mail messages, you just search for the needed information when you need it. The idea here is that "searching" replaces "filing".

I tried this approach myself and did some experimenting with it. In this experiment, I refrained from filing the finished messages in separate folders, and put them all in the catch-all folder. This is what I noticed.

For many of the messages, this approach of not filing them in separate folders worked perfectly fine. I didn't refer to these messages often anyway, and I didn't search for them often. But for the important messages that I refer to more often, searching for them didn't end up to be as easy as I thought. In many cases, I had to go through several tries to find a message, and sometimes I just couldn't find it.

The search function may be accurate and fast, but we may not know exactly what we are searching for, or we may not be able to formulate the exact search words or expressions that would locate the specific message we are looking for. In these situations search is likely to yield a result set that is time consuming to go through, or it may take several tries, and the whole process may be quite distracting and tiring as our mind scans through irrelevant messages and gets pulled in all different directions.

In addition, there is one crucial element that is lost when we rely only on search, to find important information, instead of filing this information and being able to view it all together in the relevant folder. When important messages that relate to the same topic or issue are all together, especially when they were hand picked and placed together intentionally and intuitively, those messages tell a story. This story is partially lost when we only view small pieces of it in separate searches.

In conclusion, this brings us back to the 80/20 rule. It is likely that the 80/20 rule, and the related filing strategy we discussed earlier will produce the best results. This means filing the core messages into a well designed filing structure while moving the rest of the messages to the catch-all folder. Then depending on the situation on hand, we can either use search or refer to the appropriate folders, whichever seems more appropriate and likely to yield better results. This hybrid approach is likely to capitalize on the search capabilities we have at our disposal, combined with the strategic and intuitive thinking that we put into filing our core messages.

Filing flagged messages

One aspect we haven't addressed yet is filing flagged messages after you are finished with them. After you reply to a flagged message, the idea is to file it, and when doing so, apply the same concept that we discussed earlier. This means 80/20 thinking.

The For Follow Up search folder is setup by default to display all flagged messages in our mailbox, and not just the inbox. This means that when you file a flagged message into the catch-all folder, or your other folders, it will remain visible in the For Follow Up search folder. You can easily fix this by right-mouse clicking on the For Follow Up search folder, and selecting Customize, which opens the Customize "For Follow Up" window:

Figure 13: Customize the For Follow-Up folder

You can see that currently the For Follow Up search folder includes the entire Mailbox in the search. However if you click on the Browse button, you will be able to uncheck the mailbox, and instead check the inbox folder only:

Figure 14: Limit the For Follow-Up folder search to the inbox

Once you confirm these changes by clicking the Ok button, the changes will be applied. From now on, once you drag a message from the For Follow Up search

---

folder into the catch-all folder or other folders, it will no longer be visible in the For Follow Up search, exactly as you would normally expect.

Archiving Messages

Over time, the catch-all folder, and sent items folder, as well as the rest of your folders, are going to grow in size, and you may exceed the size limit in place by your IT organization. This can be solved by periodically archiving your messages. Archiving can also be setup to automatically execute every so often. In either case, the archived messages are moved from the mailbox or current data file into a separate data file. They remain however easily accessible in the new data file and in addition they remain organized based on the same filing structure that you created before archiving. It is highly recommended to explore the archiving capabilities and setup an archiving process for your mailbox.

How about the 2000 messages in my inbox?

"But what do I do with the 2000 messages that I have in my inbox right now?" ask some of our participants. It seems that many e-mail users gave on filing e-mails and ended up leaving the message in the inbox. So for them, implementing the above techniques would involve going through these old messages and filing them or flagging them. This can be a showstopper for most people because there is barely enough time to handle current e-mail, not to mention going back in time and handling past e-mails.

Here is the practical solution: Select a cut-off date that is a few weeks back. Then move all the messages that are in your inbox and that are older than the cut-off date into the catch-all folder. It is likely that you will rarely, if ever, need to go back and review these messages, but if you do, you know where to find them. And when you refer back to a message that you think could be important for future reference, you can then move it to the appropriate folder.

Go through the remaining messages in your inbox and process them based on the above techniques. In other words, flag the ones that still require a reply and/or action, and file the ones that are finished, either in the catch-all folder, or in the appropriate folder.

From ad-hoc and overwhelming to structured and manageable

Don't get me wrong. E-mail is still going to take time to process. As long as you have coworkers, friends, and colleagues out there in the world, and as long as you have an electronic mailbox, managing e-mail will continue to be a significant activity.

However, our goal is to transform this activity from being an ad-hoc and overwhelming one, to a more structured and manageable one. We want to make e-mail a repeatable task.

In this chapter, we built the foundation for better e-mail management, and in the next couple of chapters, and later in the chapter on interruptions, we will complete the rest of the structure, and show how we can better integrate e-mail into the rest of our day, and make it not only a repeatable task, but also a contained task. Later in the book we will discuss collaboration technologies, such as blogs, wikis, and Microsoft SharePoint, and show how these technologies can help teams and organizations share information and collaborate on projects and initiative while taking the load off of e-mail.

Our ultimate goal is not to let e-mail be out of control or even worse be in control. We don't want to allow anyone who happens to be on the internet derail our train of thought and take up our precious time. We want to get e-mail well under control and stay focused on what is important.

And now you are ready to proceed with the next chapter, moving into how best we can manage our workflow and get a better handle on our calendar, to-do lists, and outstanding e-mails.

Action Plan

Identify the action items that you would like to take as a result of what was covered in this chapter. Indicate the timeframe in which you plan on taking these actions. Then report on the actual date in which you implemented them and a brief note about the results.

Table 1: Action Plan

Practice/Technique	I will start implementing this on (date?)	Actual start date	Actual end date	Comment/Results
Creating the catch-all folder and using it				
Flagging messages as described in this chapter				
Creating the flag filter in your inbox				
Referring to the For Follow Up folder to see outstanding messages				
Immediately filing messages or moving them to catch-all				
Add your own item:				
Add your own item:				
Add your own item:				

Chapter 5: Every Day Is A Complete Day—reconcile at the end of each day

In this chapter, I will introduce the end of day reconciliation process, which consists of three important activities that need to be handled at the end of the day. This doesn't have to be exactly at the end of the day, but as close to the end of the day as possible. Some users even prefer to do the end of day reconciliation in the mid to late afternoon because their end of day gets too hectic.

First End-of-Day Activity: Reconciling the red flagged messages

As we established in the previous chapter, when we go through our e-mail inbox, the messages we cannot handle right away but need to be handled today, are assigned red flags. The first activity in the end of day reconciliation consists of addressing these messages. We need to open the For Follow Up search folders, go through the red flagged messages and reply, taking actions on them as necessary:

!	🗋	🖉	From	Subject	Received	Size	In F...	▽
			Flag Status: Red Flag (12 items)					
		📨	Jim Gary	Follow-up on conversation at the event	Tue 10/12/...	5 KB	Inbox	▽
		📨	Delora Briggs	Connectivity via internal Network	Tue 10/12/...	7 KB	Inbox	▽
		📨	Carol Hagen	I am almost done with the finances	Tue 10/12/...	4 KB	Inbox	▽
		📨	Carol Hagen	One more time	Tue 10/12/...	4 KB	Inbox	▽
		📨	William Coyte	Getting ready	Tue 10/12/...	4 KB	Inbox	▽
!		📨	Crystal Renner	More slides relating to style	Tue 10/12/...	4 KB	Inbox	▽
		📨	Billy Swansan	More features for next release	Tue 10/12/...	4 KB	Inbox	▽
		📨	Delora Briggs	Meeting, Tue 5/11 or Thu 5/13, need confirmation	Tue 10/12/...	5 KB	Inbox	▽
		📨	Chris Enly	February money transfer needed by 2/10	Tue 10/12/...	5 KB	Inbox	▽
		📨	Chris Enly	Contract Incomplete	Tue 10/12/...	4 KB	Inbox	▽
		📨	Daniella Broc...	Partner Directory and Related CDs	Tue 10/12/...	7 KB	Inbox	▽
		📨	Daniella Broc...	More about the fields in the marketing database	Tue 10/12/...	6 KB	Inbox	▽

Figure 1: For Follow-up Search Folder

The no-way-out attitude

Handling the red flags needs to be approached with the no-way-out attitude. Following the no-way-out attitude, you avoid any distractions, any excuses, and stay focused on this activity until you're done.

The no-way-out attitude is necessary because most of us tend to get lost in e-mail in so many ways. We get easily distracted as we go through e-mail. We think about peripherally related issues and our mind wanders to other areas. We take mental detours and even undertake other tangent activities, and as a result e-mail becomes a slow and inefficient activity.

In addition to distractions, we avoid facing difficult issues and making difficult decisions. We may be afraid to state our opinion, to be wrong or be held responsible, or to say no to people. As a result, we tend to gravitate towards the path of least resistance, and therefore handle the easy e-mail messages and leave the difficult ones till later, keeping them postponed indefinitely.

The end-of-day reconciliation and no-way-out attitude to the rescue

The fact that the end-of-day reconciliation is towards the end of the day (and that we have limited time left) helps prompt us to stay focused. Knowing that the end of day is in sight, and that we have something to look forward to, we are likely to stay motivated.

In addition, the no-way-out attitude helps us avoid putting off the difficult issues and making important decisions. When we face issues and make the decisions, fascinating things start to happen.

First, we gain self-confidence. We set an important precedence. Our mind learns that "if we are able to solve this issue, then we will be able to solve similar issues in the future". Second, we gain experience. We learn new information and potentially new skills which we can apply in the future. Third, we gain time. Instead of issues being held in our inboxes and slowing down our progress and the progress of our team, we release them and move projects and initiatives forward.

If you want to accomplish more in less time, less effort, and less stress, start by facing the issues. Not only you will save time and effort, but you will be able to capture windows of opportunities while they are open. Later in the book, we have a lot more to say about facing pending issues, but for now, let us proceed with the mechanics of the end of day reconciliation.

Second End-of-Day Activity: Reconciling today's calendar

What comes next in the end of day reconciliation process is the calendar. Let us consider this example of today's calendar:

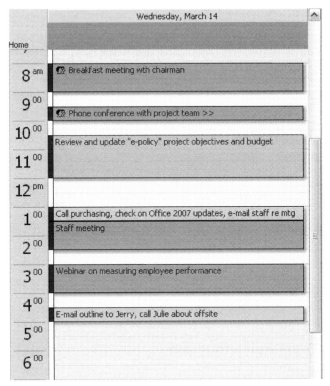

Figure 2: Today's Calendar

Before we start the reconciliation process, I would like to point out that this calendar uses color codes as follows:

a) Red indicates that this appointment or meeting is fixed and cannot be easily changed—usually involving others or even initiated by others.

b) Blue indicates a time slot that we reserved for a certain task or activity—usually self-appointed and more flexible.

c) Yellow indicates follow-ups or other to-do items that we would like to take care of at the designated time.

Reconciling the calendar consists of reviewing each item and determining if this item took place or not (in the case of a meeting), or if this item was completed or not (in the case of a task or follow-up). If the meeting did not take place, or the task or to-do item was not completed, then we need to decide what to do about it. This can involve rescheduling the meeting, or reserving time for the task at a later date, or updating someone about the status of the item, or some other action that is appropriate.

In other words, reconciling the calendar, signifies closing the loops. Closing the loops is the foundation for success in the workplace and elsewhere. Without this process, we end up with chaos. Items may remain undone and fall through the cracks. Deadlines are missed and expectations are not met. A constant feeling of being out-of-control and falling behind tends to prevail.

Let us demonstrate the calendar reconciliation process in more detail. Obviously in this demonstration, we will be explaining the details of what we are doing and the underlying concepts, therefore this process is going to appear to be slow and time consuming. In reality, this process should take just a few minutes, sometimes a little longer depending on the complexity of the issues that you deal with. Most importantly, as you establish the end-of-day reconciliation as a daily routine, you will become better at it, and get it done in no time.

Calendar reconciliation demonstration

Let us start with the first item on the calendar, the breakfast meeting. I have had this breakfast meeting, so I am going to include a visual cue indicating that it took place by adding X next to it.

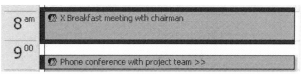

Figure 3: Breakfast meeting took place

Adding the visual cue is an optional step. You can alternatively just skip it and go to the next item on the calendar. However, the visual cue provides several benefits. When you look back at your calendar, for future reference, you will know with confidence that the item took place. Also during the reconciliation process, it helps you quickly see where you are, as you flip back and forth to other days on the calendar, or between the calendar and other applications. In addition, some users like it because it gives them the feeling of accomplishment, similar to crossing off items on a to-do list.

The phone conference also took place, so I am going to indicate so:

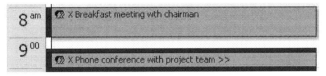

Figure 4: Conference call took place

The next item represents a task that I intended to accomplish during the designated time period: "Review and update e-policy project objectives and budget". While I started to work on this task, I did not completed it. I would like to find another time slot to finish this task, preferably tomorrow knowing that this task is due this week. Looking at tomorrow's calendar, I find an afternoon time slot and reserve the time to complete the task:

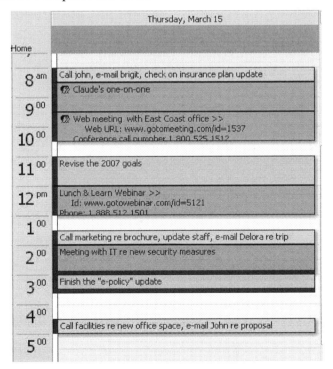

Figure 5: "Finish e-policy update" added to tomorrow's calendar

Now back to today's calendar, I would like to add a visual cue to the "Review and update e-policy project objectives and budget" task to indicate that this was reconciled. In this case, I might use a different visual cue (like WIP which stands for Work-In-Progress) to indicate that this task was not completed:

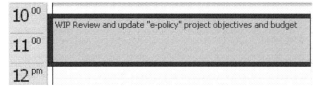

Figure 6: Item marked as reconciled even though in this case not complete

So, now it is going to get more interesting. I am at the next item which consists of "Call purchasing, check on office 2007 update, e-mail staff regarding meeting".

As you can see, this item represents various follow-ups and to-do items that I intended to do. Let us take a look at them and follow the same logic as before, by adding the visual cue next to the ones that are done. I did call purchasing, so I will add X next to it:

Figure 7: Item marked as reconciled

Let us now consider the "check on office 2007 update" item. This item has been on my calendar for several days, and even though I keep intending to do it, I find myself postponing it day after day. As a result, I am coming to the realization that for the time being, I have other more important priorities, and I won't be able to get this item done in the near future. Based on this realization, and knowing that this item is not time sensitive, I would like to "demote" it – take it off my calendar.

However, when demoting it, I don't want to completely forget about it, or have it hanging in the background of my mind, taking up precious mind space and energy. This is an opportunity to introduce one of the most valuable tools and important concepts which we call the catch-all to-do list.

The catch-all to-do list is intended to be a "parking lot" for the myriad of to-do items that come our way, which don't have a specific time frame associated with them. Instead of having these scattered on post-it-notes, or other paper or electronic formats, the idea is to consolidate them into one place in the catch-all to-do list. The catch-all to-do list can be in any format and reside in any medium that work best for you. It can be electronic such as an Outlook task list, an Excel spreadsheet, or a Word document, or even a paper notebook.

Catch-all to-do list example

In this example, we will be using a Microsoft Word document to store our catch-all to-do list. In this document, I have a table of contents that includes some broad categories such as Actions, Calls and emails, Errands, Voice messages, Waiting for, Some day, and Ideas:

To-Do List.doc - Microsoft Word

File   Edit   View   Insert   Format   Tools   Table   Bluebeam   Window   Help   Type a

To-Do List

Actions

Follow-up with Webmater radio and Susan Smith
Find out about Ajax
Call AT&T and add Caller ID
Check on dell warranty and fixing the dell computers
Find out more about this book publishing company (http://www.happyabout.info)
Review notes from Tom Drews' Webinar on effective webinars
Setup the weekly announcement to be sent automatically
Order the smaller notebooks

Calls/E-mails

Call John about salesforce.com
Call Mike and follow-up with him
Call Samantha, Donna's assistant, at 800.822.1200
E-mail Bill about the symphony

Errands

Buy Post-It-Notes
Buy Printer Paper

Figure 8: Catch-all to-do list using Microsoft Word

This table of contents is clickable. If I want to see the Someday items, I press the control key and at the same time click on Someday in the table of contents. This takes me to the Someday section in the document. This makes the catch-all to-do list easy to navigate.

When adding items to the catch-all to-do list, I apply one of the concepts we introduced earlier in the book, which is "the most recently used goes on top". For instance, in the case of the "check on office 2007 update" item, I first decide which category it belongs to, and then add it as the top item in this category. In this case, let us say this is an action, so I add it to the Actions category:

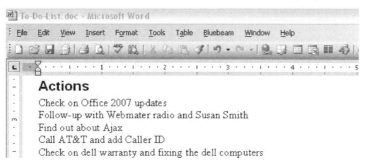

Figure 9: Adding items to catch-all to-do list

The catch-all to-do list is a semi-ordered list

Remember the concept of distance that we introduced earlier in the workbook. According to that concept, we try to keep some distance between the time we are faced with information and the time we invest in organizing it. The catch-all to-do list subscribes to the "distance" concept very well. It is categorized which gives us some degree of easy navigation and access, but yet, within each category, items are not ordered. New items within each category are placed on top. This makes the catch-all to-do list efficient and allows us to manage large numbers of items without a substantial time investment into ordering and arranging those items.

Customizing your catch-all to-do list

The categories shown in the sample catch-all to-do list discussed above are probably useful for most of us. In addition, you are encouraged to add the categories that you need based on your work environment and preferences. The possibilities are endless and the sky is the limit. Below is an example of how one manager customized the catch-all to-do list to fit her needs.

Joanne happens to manage a group of five employees and has meetings with each of them periodically to discuss projects, performance goals, and administrative issues. During a typical day, Joanne encounters issues relating to her staff, or comes up with thoughts and ideas that needed to be discussed with them. Sometimes the issues are urgent and require immediate attention, but often the issues are not urgent and can be discussed the next time she happens to talk to them or meet with them.

Joanne created a category called staff in her catch-all to-do list, and within this category she created a sub-category for each employee:

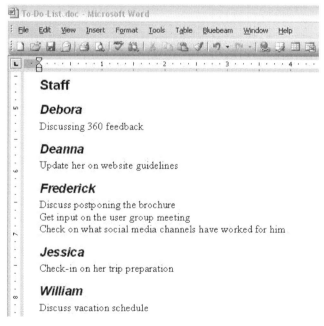

Figure 10: Staff category and sub-categories

When Joanne encounters an issue that she would like to discuss with Frederick for instance, she clicks on Fredrick in the clickable table of content, and then adds the issue to Fredrick's list.

When Joanne has a one-on-one meeting with Fredrick, or if she happens to talk to him unexpectedly, she goes through the list. Joanne may even use the catch-all to-do list to quickly document the result of their discussion. This list also servers as a log for future reference, providing continuity from week to week.

Joanne's example is just one way the catch-all to-do list application can be broadened to help consolidate a variety of issues, easily and efficiently, without spending too much time organizing and prioritizing. After all, in today's information overload, who has time to organize and prioritize? And most importantly, shouldn't the precious time we have be focused on our core activities?

The general philosophy of Accomplishing more with less is that organization shouldn't be a task by itself. Organization should be "transparent". Ideally it is done automatically and the minimal time spend doing it needs to bring immediate return on investment – a concept that we will come back to throughout this book.

How long and how often?

The catch-all to-do list can get quite long. After all if you are a busy professional, you are likely to be bombarded by all kinds of issues that need to be captured. If you don't capture them in one consolidated area, they are likely to take over your desk, your computer, your wall, your floor, and your mind.

Philip saw his list become a very long document over time and he became concerned, thinking that he was falling behind. After discussing his concerns and reviewing his list in more detail, he came to the realization that the catch-all to-do list is not meant to be fully completed and concluded like a traditional to-do list.

Some of the issues which were captured ended up proving to be not as important as originally thought (the concept of distance) and didn't need to be done. In other cases, the requirements or scope of the project, or his responsibilities in certain areas, changed and the related items in the catch-all to-do list were no longer applicable.

Another concept that helped Philip feel more at ease with his long catch-all to-do list was the 80/20 rule. Philip realized that in reality, he could not possibly complete all the items in the catch-all to-do list. There was just not enough time. The only way to cope with that was to be selective and choose the activities that were going to have the highest impact on his results. This prompted Philip to do some more strategic thinking and focus his effort on these activities.

You can even take this discussion a step further and consider adding the Not-To-Do category to the catch-all to-do list, and then consciously move items that are not likely to have high impact on results to this category and therefore not do them. When you do this, you feel relieved and empowered. Saying no, not the casual no but the strategic no, is one of the behaviors that will help you accomplish the most. Of course, in some cases, when you deicide not to do an item, you may have some negotiation to do, and we will get to that when we talk about managing priorities and results in the upcoming chapters.

In conclusion, think of the catch-all to-do list as a choice list and not a traditional to-do list. It is intended to a) release your energy from being preoccupied by these uncaptured or loosely captured tasks and to-do items, b) save you time so you are not prematurely organizing and prioritizing these items, and c) give you an good overview of these items so you can act on them more strategically and decide what to do and what not to do.

The as-needed-basis concept

So how often do you review the catch-all to-do list? It is all up to you, and depends on the types of items that you decide to capture in the catch-all to-do list and on your personal preferences.

John decided to include in the catch-all to do list even short term items, and therefore review the list daily as part of his end-of-day reconciliation process. Christine includes only items that don't have a specific deadline or timeframe associated with them, and therefore reviews the list every week or so. Paul reviews the list even less frequently and usually only when he think that such a review is necessary (on an as-needed-basis).

This as-needed-basis concept is yet another important concept in the accomplishing more with less methodology. This methodology requires that you incorporate a few simple concepts such as the end of day reconciliation, and the beginning of day reconciliation which we will discuss in the next chapter. The rest is all up to you and in most cases can follow the as-needed-basis concept.

When you review the list, usually you will find yourself crossing off many items because they were already completed or because they are no longer applicable. You will also find yourself acting on certain items and getting them completed right away, or moving them to the calendar, and therefore assigning to them a specific target completion date.

Back to calendar reconciliation

Now that we have "demoted" the "check on office 2007 update" item to the catch-all to do list, this is how today's calendar looks like:

Figure 11: Item has been moved to the catch-all to-do list

The next item is the "email staff regarding meeting". I did not get a chance to e-mail the staff, so I am going to take a few minutes and get this done now, and then indicate that I have done it.

As you can see, the reconciling time is also action time. It is the time to finish some of the follow-up items that you wanted to do during the day but hadn't yet done. In reality, reconciliation time can be your most productive time. Once you get into it, you gain momentum, and become faster at processing these items and completing those that are still outstanding.

Now, moving to the next item on today's calendar, the staff meeting took place, so I'm going to cross that off.

I was not able to attend the webinar on measuring employee performance, so I am going to reschedule it. Again, I might visit the webinar provider website now and reschedule it for another day, and then adjust my calendar accordingly.

Finally, I am going to e-mail the outline to Jerry now, and then cross this item off.

I didn't call Julie, and I prefer not to call her now, so I will move this item to tomorrow morning, adding it to the morning follow-ups, and taking it off of today's calendar.

My calendar end of day reconciliation is now complete, and my calendar looks like this:

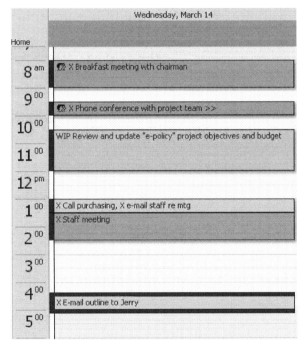

Figure 12: Today's calendar after reconciliation

Calendar reconciliation, a crucial awareness exercise

The calendar reconciliation process will end up being fast and efficient once you start implementing it and gain experience doing it.

This process has tremendous implications. Not only does it allow us to get many of our follow-up items completed, and make sure we are closing the loop on outstanding items, but it is also a crucial exercise in becoming more aware of how we spend our time and how long things really take. As a result, we get better at estimating tasks and also become more strategic in managing them, which are key factors for our success.

This process also acknowledges that we live in a very dynamic work environment, in which urgencies come up and priorities change. It is not likely that our daily activities match what we planned on our calendar. The calendar reconciliation help us account for these discrepancies by prompting us to complete some of the outstanding items and strategically reevaluate and reschedule other items.

If we resist this dynamic nature of today's work environment, we are likely to be stressed and jeopardize our success. If we surrender to it and use the calendar reconciliation to adapt and cope, we are likely to thrive. Imagine what would happen if we embrace and celebrate it and value the learning that comes with it!

Third End-of-Day Activity: Reconciling the journal

The third and final activity in the end-of-day reconciliation consists of reconciling the journal. What about the journal? Before we dive into reconciling the journal, a refresher on how we use the journal during the day might be in order.

At the beginning of each day, we start a new page in the journal. We reflect on what we "intend" to accomplish and jot down our intention for the day. Then on the next page, we reserve room to capture ideas and to-do items that didn't require immediate attention but that we want to track and process later. Then on the next page, we make room for notes. In the notes area, we capture meeting notes as well as reflect and strategize on things.

One of our workshop participants, spontaneously and with a lot of excitement, voiced a revelation she had as we discussed the journal, "so the journal is like an extension of our memory" she said. That is so true in so many ways. It is the extension of our short term memory. It gives our mind workspace to think, reflect, and strategize (the notes section). It is also the extension of our medium and long term memory, allowing us to capture ideas and to-do items which would otherwise be occupying and preoccupying our mind (the capture page). The journal is also a complete log of what happened which can be useful for future reference.

Most importantly, the journal serves as an extension of our memory by helping us declare what our intentions for the day are, and then serving as a reminder for these intentions throughout the day. The journal helps us put a stake in the ground as to what our intentions are, so we don't continue to escape them or avoid them, as our mind comes up with clever excuses, and derails us into the path of least resistance.

Let us now get into the journal reconciliation.

Reconciling Today's Page in the Journal

We will review what we intended to accomplish today, and schedule outstanding items on our calendar or occasionally capture them in the catch-all to-do list. This is also the time to feel proud of what we have accomplished. There is always so much more to be done that we normally forget to stop and appreciate what we have completed.

This is what today's intentions page might look like when reconciled:

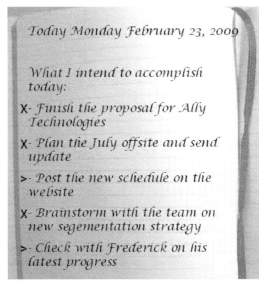

Figure 13: Today's page in the journal after reconciliation

Note that we used a visual cue similar to the one we used in calendar to indicate that an item has been completed. We also used a new notation ">" to indicate that an item has been rescheduled or moved to the catch all to-do list.

Reconciling the Capture Page in the Journal

Then we need to go through the Capture Page, review the items on this page and reconcile them. This may also be a good time to get some of these items done. Jennifer captured the following items on her Capture Page in the calendar:

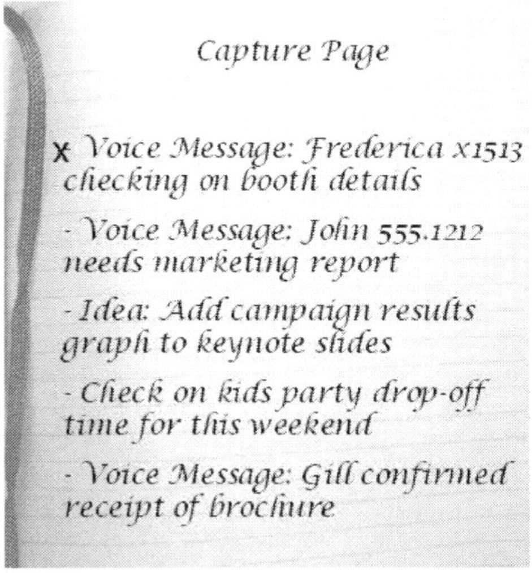

Figure 14: Capture page in the journal before reconciliation

Notice the "X" next to the first voice message from Frederica. This signifies that she already took care of this item. During the journal reconciliation, Jennifer manages to complete many of these items and move others to calendar or the catch-all to-do list as follows.

First she e-mails John the marketing report. She captures 'add campaign results to slides' in the ideas section of her catch-all to-do list. She sends a text message to her friend asking about the drop-off time for this weekend. And then, she e-mails Gill the next shipment information. Here is her Capture page now:

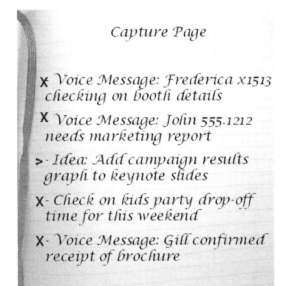

Capture Page

✗ *Voice Message: Frederica x1513 checking on booth details*

✗ *Voice Message: John 555.1212 needs marketing report*

➤ *Idea: Add campaign results graph to keynote slides*

✗ *Check on kids party drop-off time for this weekend*

✗ *Voice Message: Gill confirmed receipt of brochure*

Figure 15: Capture Page in the journal after reconciliation

There is a lot to learn from Jennifer's way of handling her Capture Page. First Jennifer uses this page not only to capture potential to-do items and ideas, but also voice messages. Capturing voice messages on this page helped her easily identify them at a glance and manage them in one place instead of having them scattered on post-it notes and papers around her desk. She can track which ones have been dealt with and which ones are outstanding, and have a log of them with the corresponding details such as telephone numbers and issues for future reference.

Note that Jennifer tracked ideas that came to her mind throughout the day by jotting them down on the Capture Page as well. When do new ideas and creative thoughts come to us? Do they come to us when we sit down and request that they do? Not usually. Our mind seems to somehow shoot them out at the least expected times and in the least favorable circumstances. If we don't capture them, they will continue to preoccupy our mind, and in some cases they can be forgotten and un-utilized. The Capture Page provides the opportunity to capture these ideas. Additionally, the catch-all to do list allows us to park them until they can be leveraged.

As you can see, the journal can be your companion throughout the day. Depending on your preference, and how large your briefcase or purse is, your journal can be the regular 8.5" x 11" size, or the 5.25" x 8.25" size, like one of the popular

Moleskine journals, or even the smaller 3.5" x 5.5" pocketsize notebook, which is another popular Moleskine journal. One journal brand that is also popular is the Levenger journal where pages can be easily added and taken out. Some of our workshop participants find numerous advantages and applications for this feature and come up with new and interesting ways of using their Levenger journals.

Paper or electronic? What is the answer?

During our workshops, we often get into a debate about why should we use a paper journal in a world that seems to be run by electronic tools. My view on this is simple. If you can accomplish the same purposes that the paper journal accomplishes using an electronic tool, and you prefer an electronic tool, go for it.

As I mentioned at the beginning of this book, the purpose of the "Accomplishing more with less" methodology is to present key concepts and let you run with them using any tools that you see fit. If for instance you think your laptop, or iPhone, BlackBerry, Treo, or Windows Mobile device can do the job, let them do it.

Advantages of the paper journal

In my experience, and the experience of many of our workshop participants, the paper journal offers three advantages over electronic tools: Speed, portability, and perspective. It takes just a few seconds, literally 5 to 10 seconds, to capture an important note in the paper journal. In the electronic world, it may take that much time, and usually much more, just to get to the application where we capture the information. Then capturing the information in an electronic tool can take more time especially if you are dealing with a small keyboard or stylus.

More often than not, we don't have much time, and most often than not, we get these great ideas or get reminded about these to-do items or issues in the middle of meetings, during phone conferences, or while we are in transition. Every second counts, especially when we want to stay connected with other people, not lose eye contact for too long, and continue to notice and observe non-verbal cues such as gestures and facial expressions. Laptops and smartphones can get in the way. A paper journal is much "quieter", less intrusive, and less demanding.

While portability of electronic gear has come a long way, and continues to with the ongoing introductions of light thin products, it will be a long time before it can compete with the paper journal which has taken portability to a whole new level. For one thing, the paper journal weighs very little, does not require any accessories, and never runs out of battery. If you choose the pocket size journal, you can almost have it with you 24x7, not to imply that this is suggested or recommended.

The most important and strategic advantage of the paper journal is perspective. We are so immersed in the electronic world that we often end up losing perspective. The journal rescues us from drowning in the ocean of electronic information, and encourages us to stay in touch with what is happening around us. It helps us focus on what is important. In addition, freely drawing in our notes page when thinking and strategizing, using arrows to link items, using our hands more naturally than finger-typing, are all likely to induce the flow of our creative juices.

In conclusion, we find the paper journal to be a great complement to the electronic tools we use everyday. It provides additional speed, portability, and perspective. It supports our information capture needs as well as serves as our thinking and strategizing pad. I recommend you find out which journal works best for you, experiment with it, and tailor your use based on your needs and preferences.

Reconciling the Notes Pages

Remember the tip I mentioned earlier in the book regarding the notes pages in the journal? I suggested that you add a checkbox (an empty square) in the left margin next to action items and items that require a follow-up of some sort. These checkboxes pay off now during the reconciliation process.

Reconciling the notes pages consists of skimming these pages quickly and looking for these checkboxes. When you find a checkbox, you can reconcile the item by taking the action now, scheduling it for later, or capturing it on the catch-all to do list. Jerry found two checkboxes today, relating to meetings he attended and managed to take the necessary actions and check them off:

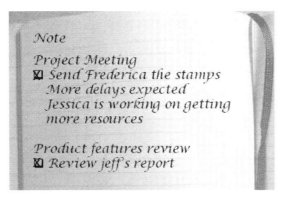

Figure 16: Journal Notes Page after reconciliation

Back to the concept of distance

The journal enables us to capture information when we are faced with it, and then process it later, mainly during the end-of-day reconciliation. This is the perfect example of the concept of distance that was presented earlier in the book. Instead of taking too much time and energy trying to figure out the importance of this information and what to do about it, we let it rest a bit, and give ourselves a chance to gain some perspective.

During the end-of-day reconciliation, we may decide that this action item or idea is not as important and as promising as it appeared when we were first faced with it. We may then transfer it to the catch-all list for the future or even cross it off permanently. When this happens, and it is likely to happen often enough, you will be happy that you didn't invest too much time and energy in this action item or idea in the first place.

How about journaling

It is a journal after all. If you are inclined to journal, or want to give this technique a try, the journal is the ideal place to do it. This can be a practice that you do on a regular basis or on an as-needed basis. Journaling about lessoned learned for example can be a powerful way to leverage them in the future. We somehow seem to skip over important lessons learned as they stay afloat in our mind and then somehow disappear. Journaling can help crystallize our learning. Journaling also helps affirm an intention to apply the learning in the future. There is a strong relationship between clear intentions and future actions. Journaling can strengthen the link between the two.

Let us take the journaling practice into yet another level. Do you want to make a change in your life but don't know where to start or still hesitating or lacking motivation? Try journaling about it on a daily basis for a week or two. Then leave it alone and see what happens. At least, you gain more clarity on the situation. At best, your commitment level increases, and you find yourself taking concrete and relevant actions knowingly and unknowingly.

Sometimes, to your surprise, after journaling about a desired change or goal, you may come to the conclusion that it isn't really what you want or not as important as you thought. You can then more peacefully let go of it instead of continuing to hold on to it.

Dare to journal! The results can be beyond your imagination.

Tracking to do items that have deadlines

During the reconciliation process, we used the catch-all to-do list to capture items that don't have a specific deadline or desired timeframe associated with them. How about those items that have a deadline or a desired timeframe? Where would we track these?

As Monique was reconciling her Capture Page in the journal, she encountered the following two items which she took note of during the day:

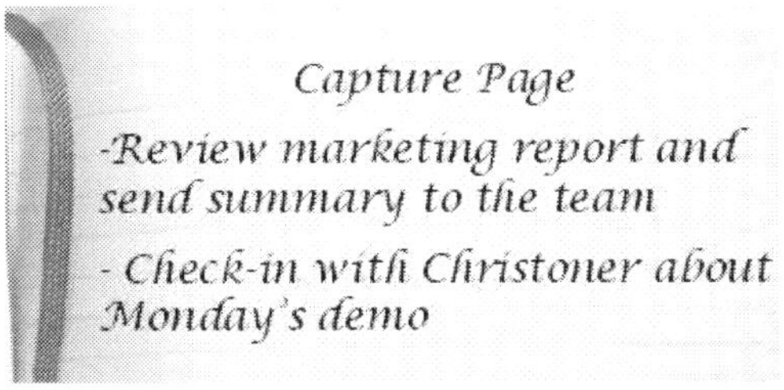

Capture Page
-*Review marketing report and send summary to the team*
- *Check-in with Christoner about Monday's demo*

Figure 17: Capture Page items to be reconciled

Reviewing the marketing report needs to be accomplished by end of day tomorrow. Monique reserves 30 minute on her calendar to review the report and send the summary to her team. Checking-in with Christopher involves a quick e-mail or phone call, and is not likely to take more than just a few minutes. Monique included this also on her calendar together with a number of other follow-ups that she already had scheduled for the early afternoon:

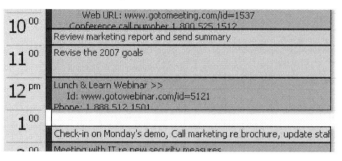

Figure 18: Capture Page items reconciled and moved to tomorrow's calendar

As you can see Monique is tracking to-do items that have a deadline or a desired timeframe on her calendar. John, another participant, decided to track such items in the task list in Outlook, and assign a priority and a due date to each one of them. While Susan opted to have a running list on a separate paper notepad dedicated to these items.

For John and for Susan, the end-of-day reconciliation process should be expanded to include their to-do lists, which we refer to as short-term to-do list to differentiate them from the catch-all to-so list. This would involve reviewing the short term to-do list, crossing off completed items, potentially adjusting the priority and due date for other items, and adding more items as necessary.

Whether you keep such to-do items on your Calendar, similar to what Monique did, or on a separate short-term to-do list, similar to what John and Susan did, is mostly a personal preference. What is important is to make sure that this list is included in the reconciliation process and well integrated with the rest of your system. It is also important to note that this list is substantially different from the catch-all to-do list and serves a different purpose. The two complement each other quite well.

If I was to recommend an approach, I would recommend Monique's approach for the following reasons. First, for to-do items that are going to take up a chunk of our time, like reviewing the report in Monique's case, having such items on our calendar helps us reserve time for them instead of allowing our calendar to be filled up with back to back meetings for instance. This technique also give us a better visual indication of how busy we are and how committed our time is, so we can easily determine how much more we can take on, and better estimate when we can get things done. In addition, it helps us solidify our intention of getting the item completed in the desired timeframe.

Having the less significant follow-up items on our calendar, such as checking-in with Christopher regarding Monday's demo, not only saves us the time of repeatedly scanning a separate to-do list, but also brings such items to the foreground, and serves as a benign reminder for these items as we scan our calendar throughout the day.

For those using Outlook 2007, you can have the best of both worlds. In Outlook 2007, the task list is well integrated with the calendar. Items on the task list are also shown in the calendar view right below their due date. In addition, you can easily re-order items or move them to a specific date and time on the calendar by simply dragging them. In this case, you can track these to-do items in the task list, and yet have the benefit of seeing them and manipulate them right from your calendar.

End-of-day reconciliation in review

The reconciliation process as outlined above included three important parts:

1) Processing the red flagged e-mails that were assigned for today

2) Reviewing today's calendar items, marking off those that were completed, and completing or rearranging those that are still outstanding

3) Reviewing today's journal pages, and completing or rearranging those items that are still outstanding

Our reconciliation process included the use of a catch-all to-do list, where we transferred items that didn't have specific deadlines or timeframes for future reference.

Items that have specific deadlines or desired timeframes were captured on the calendar. But such items can be alternatively captured in a separate short-term to-do list, which then gets reconciled as part of the end-of-day reconciliation process. We also discussed some of the advantages of using the calendar as opposed to a separate to-do list.

The reconciliation process can be one of most productive periods of our day in which we complete items that we intended to do throughout the day but couldn't. In addition, we complete items that came up unexpectedly during the day and that we captured in the journal instead of allowing them to interrupt our flow.

For some people, the end-of-day reconciliation is a 10 to 15 minute process. For others, it may be an hour or more of intense work, especially those who get one or two hundred emails per day, attend back to back meetings and phone conferences, and are dealing with many complex issues and initiatives. Having a structured end-of-day reconciliation process can help make our work efficient and rewarding instead of being overwhelming and frustrating. If you have back to back meetings all day, make it a point to cancel or delegate one of the afternoon meetings, and replace it with the end-of-day reconciliation process.

As we mentioned at the beginning of this chapter, some users feel too pressured to do the end-of-day reconciliation process right before they leave at the end of the day. It may be that many urgencies or unexpected last-minute demands come up at that time. If this is your situation, you may be more successful by scheduling a mid afternoon session instead of end-of-day session. The exact time doesn't matter. What matters is taking that time to make the reconciliation process happen.

End-of-day reconciliation, a core activity

Not only can it be one of the most productive times of our day, but it is also where the rubber hits the road. The end-of-day reconciliation process, when we view it with the no-way-out approach and an intention to get things reconciled, prompts the issues and brings them "in our face". It hands us the opportunity to do something about them, and the opportunity to learn and grow. The end of day reconciliation is not an extra chore, but a core activity, in which we get things done, and get positioned to impact the future.

Action Plan

Identify the action items that you would like to take as a result of what was covered in this chapter. Indicate the timeframe in which you plan on taking these actions. Then report on the actual date in which you implemented them and a brief note about the results.

Table 1: Action Plan

Practice/Technique	I will start implementing this on (date?)	Actual start date	Actual end date	Comment/Results
Creating the catch-all to-do list and using it				
Reserving 30 to 45 minutes for the end-of-day reconciliation				
Emptying the inbox every single day and handling red flags				
Reviewing the calendar at the end of each day				
Reviewing journal pages at the end of each day				
Add your own item:				
Add your own item:				
Add your own item:				

Chapter 6: Every Day is A Fresh Day—reconcile at the beginning of each day

How do most of us start our day? When we ask our workshop participants this question, the answer we invariably get is: "on e-mail". Here are some of the reasons why we start the day on e-mail (and why we keep going back to e-mail every time we hear the beep or when we are at a loss of what to do next):

1. Curiosity: We are curious about what happened in the world since we checked e-mail last.

2. Hope for good news: This is the winning-the-lottery syndrome. It may happen to me! I may get this great promotion or great deal or great surprise from someone.

3. Feeling accomplished: Replying to e-mails gives us the feeling that we are getting things done. Each e-mail message answered is like a micro-project successfully completed and checked off the list.

4. Fear of being left behind: We want to make sure we are not missing important information or developments, and potentially losing our competitive edge.

5. Anxiety about outstanding tasks: We cannot relax if we have outstanding e-mail messages.

6. Avoidance: Instead of focusing on more important and usually more difficult tasks, it is easier to be on e-mail.

7. Lack of direction/Need for direction: We don't know exactly what we should be doing, e-mail give us the answer, at least a temporary fix.

8. Handling urgent stuff: We have to check e-mail because we get urgent requests on e-mail, which need to be handled immediately.

9. Meeting the expectations of others: It is usually expected that e-mails are answered fairly quickly, either by our boss, colleagues, or generally as part of the culture in our organization. If we don't meet these expectations, we may be seen as "not fully on top of things".

And there are probably more reasons. All together, these factors make e-mail seductive, addictive, rewarding, and anxiety-provoking, all at the same time.

But e-mail is also our main means of communication. It allows us to do great things. The "accomplishing more with less" methodology does not blame e-mail for our inefficiencies, but it recognizes that we have developed behaviors around e-mail which, instead of fully leveraging this efficient medium, are turning it into a huge time and energy waste, and significantly increasing its cost-benefit ratio. My goal is to encourage and facilitate behavioral changes that can help you turn this around.

In this chapter, I will introduce the beginning of day reconciliation process, which also consists of three important activities that need to be handled at the beginning of the day.

First Beginning-of-Day Activity: Starting with the journal

Instead of starting the day with e-mail, how about starting it with the journal? Open your journal to a new page, and write down today's date, and then write down a brief outline of what we intend to accomplish today, as shown below:

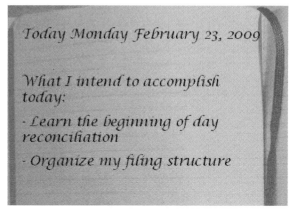

Figure 1: Today's Page--what I intend to accomplish today

Then start the Capture Page, and again as we explained in the journal chapter, use this page to jot down to-do items and ideas that you encounter throughout the day, and that you don't want to handle immediately, but rather capture and handle at a time when it is more convenient.

Figure 2: Capture Page

And finally, start the "Notes" page, where you capture meetings notes, phone conversion notes, thinking and strategizing notes.

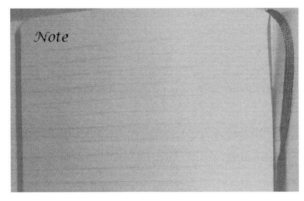

Figure 3: Notes Page

One common question we get in the workshop is: "Why do I need to write down what I intend to accomplish today when I already have these items on my calendar, or my to-do list?"

If you are comfortable with what is on your calendar and/or to-do list, and feel that they adequately represent what you want to accomplish today, then you can skip this step. However, before you decide to skip this step, continue reading and make your decision later.

Here are some of the advantages of stopping, reflecting, and writing down what we intend to accomplish today in the journal:

1. There are strong forces constantly pulling us towards leading a "robotic" work life highly driven by e-mail, instant messaging, meetings, and an array of interruptions, mostly outside our control. Stopping and reflecting on what we want to accomplish each day is our antidote to this interruption driven out-of-control existence. It is the first and necessary step we need to take if we are to exercise some degree of control over our destiny, if we want to be more purposeful, and channel our energy into the right places.

2. We tend to be driven by structured data, and there is plenty of it around to keep us busy, but then we lose touch with our intuitive thinking. Our intuition is likely to have rich information and valuable insights that we are not leveraging. When we stop to reflect on what we want to accomplish today we create just enough space to allow our intuition to surface and help us make better decisions about what we should be focusing our energy on now.

3. We live in a very dynamic world. It has been said, and rightfully so, that the only element that doesn't change is change itself. Our calendar and to-do list are relatively static. As soon as we put items on our calendar or to-do list these items are already outdated at least to some degree, because the world has already changed, at least a bit, and sometimes even drastically. Only by stopping and reflecting, we can realize more fully what has changed, and be in a position to make the necessary adjustments, and take better actions.

Being purposeful, listening to our intuition, and constantly adjusting to an ever changing world, are imperative measures that can help us accomplish more in less time, less effort, and less stress, and lead happier work and personal lives. Starting our day by writing down what we intend to accomplish today is a powerful way to unleash these forces and put them into gear each and every day.

How long does it take?

Reflecting on what we intend to accomplish today and jotting it down can be quick and easy on certain days, while it may be more involved on other days. This depends on the nature of the issues we are dealing with at the moment, the phase we are at in our projects and initiatives, the level and scope of our roles and responsibilities, among other things.

This process however is supposed to be relatively quick. We are talking about minutes here, and ideally no more than ten or fifteen of them (just enough to give us a chance to identify what is important for today, and help align our actions with what is truly going on in the world around us). These minutes are a small investment compared to the enormous returns.

Second Beginning-of-Day Activity: Reconciling the calendar

Now that we have purposefully defined what we want to accomplish today, it is time to take a look at our calendar, get mentally prepared for the day, and potentially make adjustments based on what we intend to accomplish today.

As Susan stopped and reflected on what she wanted to accomplish today, she remembered the project meeting she participated in yesterday, and some of the comments that were made by the project team. She realized that there might have been some unspoken concerns among the project team members and that some important issues weren't fully handled. Susan added one more item on her journal page relating to this project:

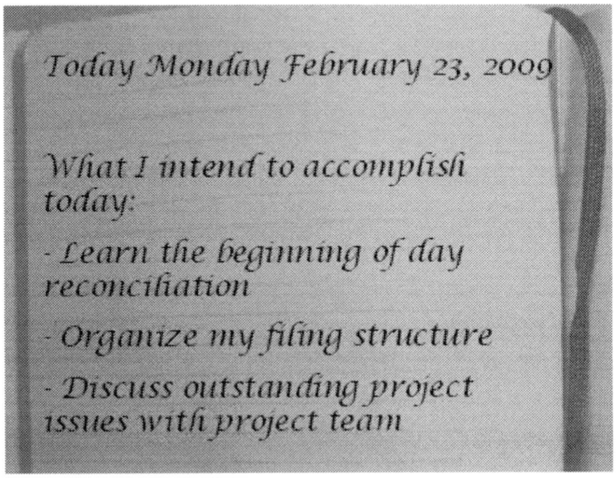

Today Monday February 23, 2009

What I intend to accomplish today:
- Learn the beginning of day reconciliation
- Organize my filing structure
- Discuss outstanding project issues with project team

Figure 4: Additional item added to Today's Page

Then when reconciling her calendar, Susan scheduled a conference call with the key project team members, and to make room for this conference call, she had to postpone another meeting. This has helped Susan and the project team proactively address some project and personnel issues which would have otherwise become difficult to manage bottlenecks and showstoppers.

Third Beginning-of-Day Activity: Handling Blue and yellow flagged messages

The third part of the beginning-of-day reconciliation relates to e-mail. Knowing that we already handled the red flagged messages when we did yesterday's end-of-day reconciliation, our goal now is to handle the blue and yellow flagged messages.

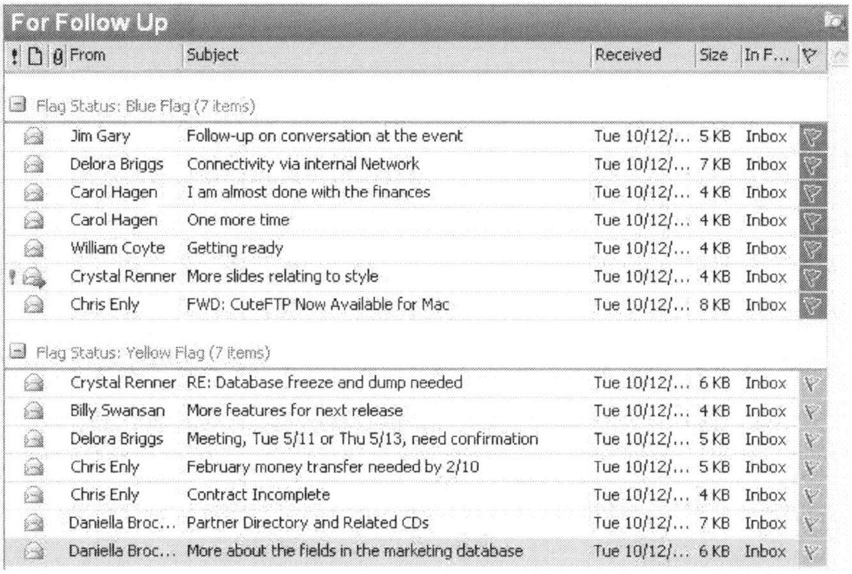

Figure 5: Blue and Yellow Flags

As I go through the blue and yellow flags, I try to immediately handle the ones that I can easily handle, assign red flags to the ones that are becoming more urgent and that I would like to handle later today, and leave the rest with their blue or yellow flags for later.

The question is: "Do I need to come back to these blue and yellow flags later today?" The answer is a definite no. By definition these messages are messages that don't require a reply or an action today. That is why we assigned them the blue or yellow flags in the first place, and that is why we left them as is when we reviewed them during the beginning-of-day reconciliation process.

Using the blue and yellow flags technique is an important boost to our productivity. If we don't assign blue and yellow flags to these messages, they would otherwise be scattered throughout our inbox in disguise, appearing to be more important and more urgent than what they really are. Not only would they be in the way, hiding more important messages, but they would likely cause us to stop and think about them again and again taking up precious time and energy. The blue and yellow flags help us take the "mask" off these messages and be clear once and for all on when we will handle them. The beginning-of-day reconciliation assures that they are reviewed periodically and handled as necessary.

And now into the inbox

Now is the time to get into the inbox and go through new messages. We will handle the urgent ones and the ones that can be easily and quickly handled, while assigning the appropriate flags to other messages.

Some workshop participants tell us that they must start their day by reviewing the inbox, as opposed to the beginning-of-day reconciliation process we described above, because they get urgent messages overnight or early morning which may need immediate attention or may change how they plan the day. This usually applies to customer service, support, and sales related functions. If this is the case, you may tailor your beginning-of-day reconciliation process to include checking urgent messages first (whether e-mail or voice mail or whatever way they get to you), and then going through the steps outlined above. Be careful though, once you are in the inbox, there is an overwhelming temptation to open messages of all kinds, and find yourself two hours later still in the inbox.

Beginning-of-day reconciliation in review

The beginning-of-day reconciliation process may take 5 or 10 minutes on certain days and for some people, and longer on other days and for other people. This

---

time however is not time spent, it is time invested with same-day tenfold return on investment. Writing down what we intend to accomplish today helps us, consciously and subconsciously, stay on track throughout the day. It helps us put the stake in the ground and hold ourselves accountable. It also gives us the opportunity to rethink our calendar and take action to influence what is going on for us and around us. Finally, our blue and yellow flags save us significant time and energy that would otherwise be wasted throughout the day. Most importantly, the beginning of day reconciliation creates the state of mind and state of being that we need in order to lead a more productive and happy day.

Action Plan

Identify the action items that you would like to take as a result of what was covered in this chapter. Indicate the timeframe in which you plan on taking these actions. Then report on the actual date in which you implemented them and a brief note about the results.

Table 1: Action Plan

Practice/Technique	I will start implementing this on (date?)	Actual start date	Actual end date	Comment/Results
Start a new page in the journal and write what I intend to accomplish today				
Review my calendar at the beginning of the day and make adjustments if necessary				
Review my blue and yellow flags and handle or escalate those that require attention				
Add your own item:				
Add your own item:				
Add your own item:				

Chapter 7: Radically Fast Filing—file information easily and find it instantly

Most business professionals are overwhelmed by the amount of information they have to handle. They spend a significant amount of time trying to manage it and then searching for it when they need it.

When we have a well designed filing structure, we are likely to be able to file information faster and find it faster. But there is more to it. A well designed filing structure helps us think more clearly about our priorities and stay focused on what is important, as we will see shortly.

Sample Filing Structure

When it came to filing e-mail, Christine did not do much. She left her e-mails in her inbox, and then moved all the messages to an archive folder on a yearly basis. Her e-mail filing structure was as follows:

E-mail Folders

Inbox
Outbox
Sent Items
Deleted Items
Archives
   Archive Jan to Dec 08
   Archive Jan to Dec 07
Junk E-mail
Maybe Later

Figure 1: E-mail filing structure

Her hard drive structure on the other hand took a life of its own. Christine kept adding folders in an ad-hoc fashion:

Hard Drive Folders

Finance
  Business
    Analysis
    Process
    Projections
    Tax Forms
    Templates
  Nancy
  Personal
Hiring
  CEO
  Forms
  India
  Marketing
    Marketing Director
    Marketing Managers
    VP of Marketing
  Professional Services
    Consultants
    Managers
  Recruiters
  SalesReps
    Paula
    Kenny
    Brenda
Mail
Marketing
  Conferences
    DCI Bostong
    DCI SF
    DMA LA
  Customer ROI
  Digital Postcards
  Direct Marketing
  Market Research
  Marketing Features

Marketing Plan
  Direct Marketing
  Product Marketing
  Public Relations
Marketing Programs
Partnerships
Presentations
  Company 1
  Company 2
  Etc.
Public Relations
  Agencies
  Analysis
  Presentations
Seminars
  Content
  Content Updates
  Logistics
  Evaluations
Products
  Advisory Board
  Beta Specs
  Competitive Analysis
  Customers
  Demo Scripts
  Design
  Features
  Overseas Development
Sales
  Sales Goals
  Sales Planning
  Sales Proposals
  Sales Reps
  Sales Toolkit
Strategic
  Acquisitions
  Andrew
  Company Board Meetings
    Meeting 11-01

Mgmt Meetings
  Offsite 03-01
  Weekly mtgs
  Etc.
Team Meetings
Events
Funding
Market Analysis
Org. Development
Positioning
Priorities
Thinking
Tactical
  Brown Bag Lunches
  Friday Morning Mtgs
Legal
  License Agreements
Office Move
Payroll
Performance Reviews
Roles and Goals
  Employee 1
  Employee 2
  Etc.
  Quarter 1-01
  Quarter 2-01
  Etc.
Vacations
Training
  Workshops
  Executive Education
  Brown Bags
    Effective Meetings
    Software Life Cycle
  Toastmasters
  Trips

Figure 2: Hard drive filing structure

Christine did not deal with a lot of paper. Her paper folders were as follows:

Paper Folders

Legal
Accounting
Human Resources
   Contractors
   Confidentiality Agreements
Team
   Offsite Plan
License Agreement
Signed NDA's
Blank NDA's

Sales Projections
Sample Proposals

Marketing Plan
Direct Mailing Copies
Partnerships
Resources
   Strategy Consultants
   Organizational Development

Figure 3: Paper filing structure

The New and Improved Filing Structure

To help Christine improve her filing structure, we applied three filing concepts, and the following new structure emerged:

```
             E-mail Folders

Inbox               Marketing
Outbox                Articles
Sent Items            Associations
Drafts                Competition
Deleted Items         Market Research
Archive 2008          Public Relations
Junk E-mail             Speaking Opps
Work                    Web Pubs
  Accounting        Marketing Online
    Online Vendors    Online Listings
  Vendors             Sample E-mails
    Vendor 1          Search Engines
    Vendor 2          Website
    Etc.            Products
  Administrative      Case Studies
  Content             eLearning System
    Case Studies    Prospects
    Interesting Stuff Prospect 1
    Samples           Prospect 2
  Customers           Etc.
    Customer 1      Technology
    Customer 2    Z-Personal
    Etc.            Activities
  Human Resources    Family & Friends
    Recruiting       Training & Education
  Team
    Employee 1
    Etc.
  Training
Legal
```

```
            Hard Drive Folders

Work                Marketing
  Accounting          Competition
    Online Vendors      Company 1
  Vendors               Company 2
    Vendor 1            Etc.
    Vendor 2          Market Research
    Etc.             Material
  Administrative        Product Brochures
    Forms               Price Sheets
      Fax Cover Sheet   Public Relations
      Word Templates  Marketing Online
      PPT Templates     Online Ads
  Content               Website
    Case Studies      Products
    Interesting Stuff   Case Studies
    Samples             eLearning System
  Customers           Prospects
    Customer 1          Prospect 1
      Project 1         Prospect 2
        Cost Tracking   Etc.
        Estimates     Z-Personal
        Invoices        Activiites
        Planning        Family & Friends
        <Next.Doc>      Training & Education
    Customer 2        Travel
    Etc.                Agencies
  Human Resources       Places
    Interns             Trips
    Training
  Legal
```

Figure 4: Improved e-mail filing structure   **Figure 5: Improved hard drive filing structure**

```
Paper Folders

Work                          Conferences
  Accounting                    TechLaunch 03
    Business Exp Rec.           Etc.
    Project Exp Rec.          Marketing Material
  Administrative                Postcard Info
  Content                     Seminars
  Customers                     Hotels/Rooms
    Customer 1                  Etc.
      Project 1            Products
      Project 2              Product 1
    Customer 2                Offsite
    Etc.                    Prospects
  Human Resources             Prospect 1
    Colleagues                Etc.
      Barb                  Technology
      Howard                  Computers
      Etc.                      Asset 1
    Training                    Etc.
      Leadership              Electronics
      Communications           Asset 1
      Technical                Etc.r
  Legal                     Z-Personal
    Incorporation             Activiites
    Stockholders              Family & Friends
    License Agreem.           Training & Education
  Marketing                   Travel
    Articles                    Agencies
    Associations                Places
      AMA                       Trips
      ASTD
```

Figure 6: Improved paper filing structure

Turn to a new page in the journal, write down today's date, and what you want to accomplish today which is "Organize my filing structure". Start the Capture Page to capture the myriad of items that come up during the day so they don't interrupt your flow. Then start the Notes pages to capture meeting notes.

If you review the enhanced structures shown above, and compare them with the original structures Christine had, what do you notice? Take a few minutes to jot down your observations in your journal before you read on.

Concept one: One filing structure

Review the work folder in the improved e-mail filing structure and then its subfolders. You notice that within the work folder, we have the following second-level subfolders: Accounting, Administrative, Content, Customers, Human Resources, Legal, Marketing, etc.

Now review the work folder in the improved hard drive structure, and you notice that we have the same subfolders: Accounting, Administrative, Content, Customers, Human Resources, Legal, Marketing, etc. and if you take a look at the improved paper folders, you will find the same structure.

In other words, we have "one" filing structure that is consistently applied to the three mediums (e-mail, hard drive, and paper). After all, we have the same goals and responsibilities and deal with similar information irrelevant of which medium we are working in.

When designing our "one" filing structure, there are several important top level folders to consider:

1. Customers

2. Products and services

3. Internal team

4. External audiences (partners, vendors, and suppliers)

5. Content (or knowledge-base)

6. Administrative

Most filing structures are likely to include the above folders or some variation thereof. Your customers may be internal customers if you are part of the internal helpdesk team of an organization, or they may be faculty or students if you are in an educational institution. Your content folders may be your research topics if you are part of a research team. You need to adapt these folders and label them appropriately based on your environment and preferences.

Shortly I will suggest a couple of approaches to help you define your own filing structure. For now, I would like to continue with the design concepts.

Concept two: Apply the filing structure on an as-needed basis

If you take a look at Christine's improved e-mail filing structure (in Figure 4), and carefully review the Customers folder and subfolders, and then review the Customers folder and subfolders in the improved hard drive filing structure (in Figure 5), what do you notice?

In the improved hard drive filing structure, the Customers subfolders are broken down by customer, and then by project, and within each project, there are subfolders for each area of the project, such as Cost Tracking, Estimates, Invoices, Planning, etc. In the improved e-mail filing structure however, the structure is not broken down to this granular level.

This is where concept two comes into play: Apply "one" filing structure on an as-needed basis. This means that if we don't need certain folders in a certain medium, we don't create blank folders just for the sake of consistency. But if and when the need arises, we can easily add these folders. For instance, Christine does not currently need the Cost Tracking e-mail folder, but if she starts to collaborate on cost tracking spreadsheets with a co-worker, she can easily add the Cost Tacking folder to her e-mail filing structure.

Concept three: Let each medium do what it does best

We are dealing with three different mediums here: E-mail, hard drive, and paper. The third concept states "let each medium do what it does best". Instead of having the same information handled and stored in multiple mediums, concept three calls for optimizing our usage of each medium and minimizing duplication.

What is e-mail best at? When we ask this question at our workshops, participants quickly provide the correct answer: Communication. What does our hard drive do best? The answer doesn't seem as easy in this case. Storage is what comes to almost everyone's mind. Hard drives are great at storage, but there is one thing that they are "best" at. And that is for "authoring" and "editing". It is where we create documents and where we edit documents. Finally, what is paper best at? Storage, archive, and backup are common answers, but the more accurate response is storing "originals". Our paper files are primarily for storing information that cannot be otherwise reproduced. This may include documents that have signatures, handwritten notes, or documents that came to us as paper that we cannot otherwise reproduce.

If we use each of these mediums based on what they do best, instead of using them in an ad-hoc fashion and storing the same information in multiple places, two important things will happen. First, we will have a lot less information to organize, file, and store. Second, we will have less information to search when we need it later.

Let us apply this last concept to some real-life situations. Susan likes to print certain e-mails and certain documents so that she can read them on paper instead of electronically. This give her the opportunity to get away from the computer screen, maybe even sit on a comfortable chair away from the computer, and read more carefully, flipping through the pages back and forth as she refers to different sections.

When Susan is done with the printout, what should she do with it? According to the above concept, the e-mail or the document belong to the electronic medium, and the printout is nothing but a duplicate which can be reproduced at any time. Therefore ideally, Susan will throw the printout in the recycling bin.

What if Susan jots down some notes on the printout as she reads the document? The document now becomes an original and can now be filed in the paper folders. However, if Susan transfers the handwritten notes someplace else, then the printout is a duplicate, and should be recycled.

The above example demonstrates the types of questions we want to ask ourselves as we handle information so we can more efficiently manage these mediums.

Saving Attachments?

One of today's realities is that most of us deal with a large number of attachments in our e-mail inboxes. How should we manage these attachments? Do we keep them in e-mail and let them clog our already overloaded inboxes? Do we save them on our hard drive and delete them from e-mail? How do we find them easily when we need them? Many questions arise as we think of attachments.

In order to address the core issues, we would need to explore approaches such as:

a) Instead of using e-mail to exchange documents, use collaboration technologies such as Microsoft SharePoint, wikis, and document management systems.

b) In addition, we would allow users to have large mailboxes with several gigabytes of storage and advanced search capabilities that can search within attachments.

If the above options are not yet available to you, then you might want to come up with your own strategy depending on your needs and preferences, and the parameters that are imposed by your IT organization or ISP. Here are two potential strategies to consider:

1) If mailbox size is the most pressing limitation, then save every attachment that is above 1 MB (or whatever file size is appropriate) on the hard drive or shared drive, and delete the attachment from e-mail. Now that you have a consistent filing structure, it should be easy to locate the attachment later.

2) If mailbox size is not as much of an issue, then you might consider saving the important attachments (those that belong to the core 20% of our effort which generates 80% of our results) to the hard drive and leave the rest in e-mail (until they get archived).

Exercise 1: Designing your filing structure, the top down approach

Now it is time to get to work. The goal of this exercise and the following exercise is to come up with a filing structure that best fits our needs and makes it easier to file and find information.

Use the Notes section of your notebook for this exercise. First you will come up with the top level folders of your new structure. The idea here is to take a step back, put your existing filing structure on the side for the time being, and come up with an the ideal filing structure that would best fit your needs.

So which filing structure are we talking about? Is it e-mail, hard drive, or paper? That was a trick question! Remember, it is "one" filing structure. So we need to let go of thinking about the mediums for the time being and think about "information architecture".

If you take a look at the enhanced filing structure above, you see that the top level folders under the work folder are: Accounting, Administrative, Content, Customers, Human Resources, Legal, Marketing, etc. So the question in this exercise is: "What would these folders be for you?"

Once you come up with what you think the top level folder in your ideal filing structure would be, let us address a few common issues that usually come up in the workshop.

A common question is: "How many folders should we have at the top level?" 3 folders at the top level are probably too few and 15 are probably too many. We recommend that you keep it to 10 folders or less. The top level folders are supposed to represent the important areas of our information architecture, and not be an exhaustive list of all the information we deal with.

Patrick, a project manager at a technology company, had more than 20 top level folders. When we reviewed them together, we concluded that the key projects, which he put at the top level, can be grouped together under one projects folder. If you're finding yourself with many top level folders, it is likely that some of them can be grouped under one top level folder.

Your next level folders

Once you are done with the top level folders, the next step would be to come up with the subfolders within each of the top level folders. At this point, jot down the subfolders that come to your mind, and we will get a chance to refine and complete the list later when we get to exercise 2.

At this point, we would like to go to one more level, and design the 3rd level, again, detailing only as needed, and to the level that makes sense.

A question that comes up often is: "How many levels deep should the filing structure go?" Overall, we are aiming at being minimalistic and at continuing to think 80/20. This means the fewer levels the better. However when it comes to the core areas of our business (the 20%) we want to have the levels that are necessary to categorize the information appropriately and find it efficiently. We don't want to sacrifice clarity and efficiency to cut down on levels.

Exercise 2: Designing your filing structure, the bottom-up approach

This exercise will help us finish the structure that we started in the first exercise. In this exercise, you need to print out your existing e-mail structure and use the printout as indicated below. If you happen not to file your e-mails and keep it all in the inbox, then print the filing structure of your hard drive instead, and follow the same instructions.

Using the printout, review the existing filing structure, and for each folder, determine if the folder is still in use. If not, cross it off. If it is in use, then a) decide if it needs to be renamed, and b) if it needs to be moved to a more appropriate location in the structure. This is an opportunity to rename folders clearly and consistently and most importantly to continue to evolve and refine the structure that we started in the first exercise, as illustrated in the example below.

Here is a quick example from Jenny who had the following folders in her filing structure (we are only showing the Strategic folder and its subfolders just to illustrate a few points):

Existing Folders/Subfolders

- Strategic
  - Acquisitions
  - Andrew
  - Company Board Meetings
  - Team Meetings
  - Events
  - Funding
  - Market Analysis
  - Org. Development
  - Positioning
  - Priorities
  - Thinking

Figure 7: Existing Strategic folder and its subfolders (part of the printout)

Jenny went through these folders and this is how she marked her printout:

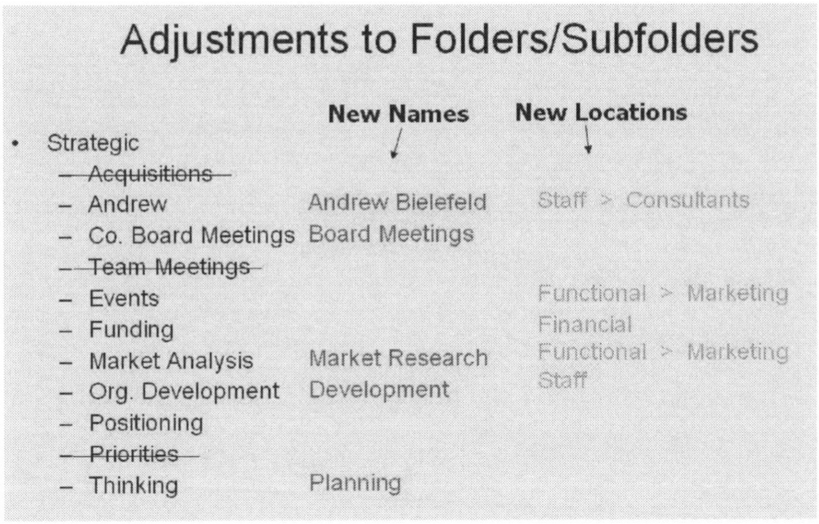

Figure 8: Adjustments made on the printout

As you can see, Jenny for instance, decided to rename the folder "Andrew" to "Andrew Bielefeld"--starting a new naming convention of using both first and last names when handling information relating to people. Then she realized that the work that she does with Andrew Bielefeld does not relate to strategic initiatives and issues and therefore should be moved to a different folder. Andrew Bielefeld is a consultant working on HR related projects so she decided to have a folder for consultants (to be named Consultants) and make it a subfolder within a top level folder for staff (to be named Staff).

At this point, Jenny took a look at the structure that she designed in exercise one above, and made sure that the folder Staff was included as a top level folder, and that Consultants was a subfolder within it. As you can see, this exercise allowed Jenny not only to clean up her old and unused folders and rename her current folder more clearly and consistently, but also to complete the design of her new and improved filing structure which we started in the previous exercise. When she completes this exercise she will have in her possession the blueprint for the new and improved filing structure.

How long does this take?

Even if you have hundreds of folders, the above exercise is not likely to take more than an hour or so. Once you get started and go through the first set of folders, it is likely that you will pick up momentum, make faster decisions and go through the folders quickly and easily. Something to keep in mind is that our goal is to simplify the structure and apply the 80/20 rule, so that the resulting structure is refined and optimized. For most business professionals, this is an opportunity to get rid of old information and unnecessary details.

How about the hard drive and the paper folders

The same exercise that we described above (going through the printout and crossing off what we don't need while renaming and deciding on the location of the folders that we need moving forward) can also be done for the hard drive filing structure. Normally most participants find it easy to do this exercise on the hard drive once they have done it on e-mail, or vice versa. Finally, you need to do this exercise for the paper folders as well.

Implementing the new filing structure

The outcome of the above two exercises is a filing structure that is up-to-date and optimized to best serve your needs. Now it is time to implement the new structure in our three mediums, based on the three concepts we discussed earlier: 1) One filing structure 2) Apply the structure on an as-needed basis, and 3) Let each medium do what it does best.

The New e-mail filing structure

This consists of creating a new top level folder in our e-mail application and calling it "Work", or "New Structure", or "New Beginning", or whatever name you find appropriate. Then we create the new filing structure within this new top level folder. Now that you have this new structure, you start using it immediately to file important e-mail messages that relate to your core activities. Remember that the less important messages can be filed in the "Catch All" folder.

What do you do with your existing e-mail folders (the ones that you had before you created the new filing structure)? The answer is simple. You put them in the Catch-All folder and then selectively move them to the new structure on an as-needed basis. This means if you find yourself referring to one of these folders, you move it to the newly created filing structure to the appropriate location based on the "blueprint" you developed in exercise two above. More often than not, participants tell us that they rarely if ever move these folders.

New hard drive filing structure

Implementing the new filing structure on the hard drive is no different than implementing it in e-mail. This consists of creating a new top level folder and then creating the new filing structure within this folder. Then you move folders and documents to the new filing structure only as needed.

New paper filing structure

Implementing the new structure in the paper folders can be more involved than the electronic world because we need to put the existing paper folders on the side to create room for the new folders. However the process is basically the same. Some users who deal with important papers find it worthwhile to go through the existing paper folders and bring the important and current documents to the new paper folders. Other users put most of the existing paper folders in storage boxes and then selectively move folders when necessary.

Frequently raised issues

Work versus personal

This question is bound to come up in every workshop and in every conversation relating to filing information: Is it best to separate work information from personal information, or keep them together? This includes items in e-mail, calendar, to-do lists, hard drive, paper folder, and the like.

We are finding that the lines between work and personal are becoming less and less defined. In today's information age, knowledge workers are finding themselves conducting business after hours, accessing their information online 24x7, and working virtually with people around the globe. Similarly, they are taking care of personal items during business hours and using their work computers, and many are finding it more convenient to keep work and personal information together.

One thing to be reminded of however is that most companies have e-policies which indicate that any information kept on company systems is subject to review by the company or is even the property of the company. E-policies also tend to restrict the amount of time that employees can spend on personal items, some being very strict, while others indicating that this time should be kept to a minimum and not interfere with the employee's ability to conduct their business activities. While companies aren't likely to review employees' personal information, if problems arise, they are likely to audit this information and use it. Employees are encouraged to use good judgment and be aware of their company's e-policy when it comes to personal use and storage of personal information.

Search versus File

This is yet another common question and relates to the issue of whether it is important to file e-mail messages, knowing that search utilities (such as Microsoft Windows Desktop Search and Google Desktop Search among others) can easily search and find information in e-mail messages and even in electronic documents when we need it.

With the e-mail volume becoming increasingly overwhelming, more users are opting not to file e-mail messages in folders, leaving messages in the inbox or archiving them into one archive area, and then using search utilities to find the information they need when they need it. Google mail application promotes this approach – which is not a surprise knowing that Google is the "search" company.

We find that this approach, of search-instead-of-file, works well when you try to find messages that fit your search criteria well. The more specifics you know about the message, the more likely search will find it quickly and easily. This approach isn't as efficient however when you only have a vague idea of what you are looking for. In this case, you may go through several searches and have to browse through several search results before you find what you want, and sometimes you may not even find it.

The approach that we recommend is a hybrid approach that leverages the best of both worlds (the "search" world and the "filing" world). This consist of filing only core message – the top 20%, and using search to find information in the remaining 80% – which meanwhile can be moved to the Catch-All folder.

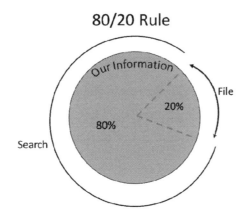

Figure 9: File 20% and use search to find 80%

The group filing structure

Many teams tend to have shared network drives and keep shared documents on these drives in order to facilitate access to these documents and better manage the process of updating these documents. The question that comes up relates to what filing structure should be used on these shared drives, and how this structure relates to individual filing structures.

We generally recommend that the team get together and follow the exercises described in this chapter to design a shared filing structure. This process can start with a brainstorming session about what the ideal filing structure would look like followed by a discussion and agreement on an initial structure (this would be similar to the first exercise in this chapter). Then the team can proceed to print the current structure of the shared drive, review it together, cross off old folders, rename folders more consistently, and decide on where folders should go in the new structure (this would be similar to the second exercise in this chapter).

As a result, the team will have a new shared drive filing structure. Then the individual team members structure can be a "super-set" of the shared filing structure in which team members add the folders that that they need for their own information that is not related to the team work.

Exercise 1: Top level folders and next level folders

For each top level folder, include the necessary 2nd level folders, and then 3rd level folders. Make copies of this form as necessary.

Table 5: Your ideal filing structure

Top Level	2nd Level (3 to 5 sub-folders within each top level folder)	3rd Level (5 to 7 sub-folders within each 2nd level)
Folder Name:	Subfolder 1 Name:	
	Subfolder 2 Name:	
	Subfolder 3 Name:	
	Subfolder 4 Name:	
	Subfolder 5 Name:	

Action Plan

Identify the action items that you would like to take as a result of what was covered in this chapter. Indicate the timeframe in which you plan on taking these actions. Then report on the actual date in which you implemented them and a brief note about the results.

Table 2: Action Plan

Practice/Technique	I will start implementing this on (date?)	Actual start date	Actual end date	Comment/Results
Designing my new filing structure				
Working with my team to come up with a structure for the shared drive				
Implementing my new filing structure in e-mail				
Implementing my new filing structure on my hard drive or network drive				
Implementing my new filing structure with my paper files				
Add your own item:				
Add your own item:				
Add your own item:				

Chapter 8: The Last Priority System You Will Ever Use— manage conflicting priorities with the "matrix"

Turn to a new page in the journal and write down today's date, and what you want to accomplish today which is "managing priorities". Start the Capture Page to capture the myriad of items that come up during the day so they don't interrupt your flow. Then start the Notes pages to capture meeting notes. We are now ready to tackle the topic of conflicting priorities and how we can best manage them.

Listing Your Immediate Priorities

On the Notes Page, list your immediate priorities – items you need to accomplish within the next two weeks. For now, this is a brain dump exercise without much thinking involved. Don't worry about ordering these items or analyzing them. Instead, any item that comes to your mind, large or small, significant project or a small to-do item, personal or work, jot it down on the journal.

The Immediate Priorities Matrix™

I am going to introduce a tool that we call the Immediate Priorities Matrix™. This is a tool you use primarily when you have too many priorities, feel overwhelmed, are not sure where to start, and concerned that you won't be able to get tasks done. They all appear to be urgent and equally important and you find yourself unable to focus on any one task and make much progress. This is exactly where the Immediate Priorities Matrix ™ comes to the rescue.

Even though our primary purpose of introducing this tool is to help you manage these challenging times, this tool is equally helpful when it comes to pre-planning. We will touch more on this topic in the following chapter.

In the exercise above, Mark jotted down the following items as his immediate priorities:

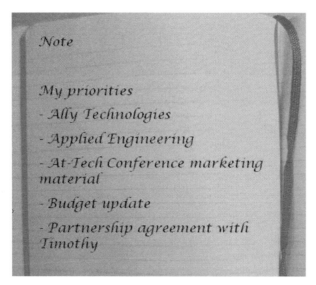

We will use the Immediate Priorities Matrix™ to help Mark better manage his priorities. The Immediate Priorities Matrix™ involves the following information organized in a table (matrix-like) format:

Table 6: Immediate Priorities Matrix™ format

Priority	Breakdown	Immediate/ Next Actions	Estimated Time	Deadline

In the first row and first column, let us put the first priority, which is one of Mark's customers (Ally Technologies):

Table 7: First priority

Priority	Breakdown	Immediate/ Next Actions	Estimated Time	Deadline
Ally Technologies				

In the second column, let us break it down into the steps that are involved in completing this priority:

Table 8: First priority breakdown

Priority	Breakdown	Immediate/ Next Actions	Estimated Time	Deadline

Ally technologies	Install new software Plan first session Update Joan & team Send material to printer Train the trainer Schedule final dates			

In the third column, let us identify the steps that are truly immediate and that need to be handled first so other steps can follow:

Table 9: Identifying the immediate

Priority	Breakdown	Immediate/ Next Actions	Estimated Time	Deadline
Ally technologies	Install new software Plan first session Update Joan & team Send material to printer Train the trainer Schedule final dates	Install new software Ask Joan for dates		

In the next column, we need to estimate how long it would take to perform the immediate steps. The final column is where we indicate the deadline or target completion date for the immediate steps.

Table 10: Estimating duration and identifying timeframe

Priority	Breakdown	Immediate/ Next Actions	Estimated Time	Deadline
Ally technologies	Install new software Plan first session Update Joan & team Send material to printer Train the trainer Schedule final dates	Install new software Ask Joan for dates	60 min 5 min	Wednesday March 21

Mark completes the matrix by filling in one row for each of his immediate priorities. As a result his Immediate Priorities Matrix™ is as follows:

Table 11: Completed Immediate Priorities Matrix™

Priority	Breakdown	Immediate/ Next Actions	Estimated Time	Deadline
Ally technologies	Install new software Plan first session Update Joan & team Send material to printer Train the trainer Schedule final dates	Install new software Ask Joan for dates	60 min 5 min	Wed Mar 21
Applied Engineering	Prepare the content Debrief Christy Update proposal Schedule call with Training director	Prepare the content first pass E-mail Christy	60 min 20 min	Tue Mar 20
Ad-Tech Conference marketing material	Finish the program outline and description Send it to conference coordinator for review Ask Christine to proof it Send to printer	Finish outline and description Send it to conference coordinator	60 min 10 min	Fri Mar 23
Budget update	Review latest input Update sales projections Finalize new hosted services agreements Send to Joan for her input	Plan what is needed, who will be contributing to this process, and delegate accordingly	2 hours	Thu Mar 22
Partnership agreement with Timothy	Review agreement with legal Update marketing material based on latest discussion Send to Christine to proof and layout Finalize and sign agreement	Update Timothy, and ask for an additional week	5 min	Thu Mar 15

A sigh of relief

At this point in time, and once the Immediate Priorities Matrix™ is filled out, participants experience a sigh of relief. When we put the above items on paper, as opposed to leaving them floating or racing in a disorderly fashion in our mind, we feel better and we are in a much better position to deal with them. In addition, breaking things down into smaller components can help us plan and execute more efficiently.

Furthermore, the Immediate Priorities Matrix™ goes a step further, and includes a deadline or target date for the immediate or next action items, which enables us to move forward to systematically schedule these immediate action items as we will demonstrate shortly. This frees us from the paralysis or frenzy that we may experience when we are faced with these priorities all at once.

Stopping and preparing the Immediate Priorities Matrix™ is a powerful response to the madness that may be going on around us. It gives us the desperately needed opportunity to notice what is really going on and reflect on it. It also lays the foundation needed to determine what to do now and what to do next. This is a very empowering exercise which gives us a sense of being in control instead of feeling driven uncontrollably by the waterfall of external circumstances.

From matrix to calendar

Our work with the Immediate Priorities Matrix™ is far from over. Actually, it has just begun. What we have done so far is the prep work and now it is time to put the Immediate Priorities Matrix™ into use. The next step is to schedule the items from the "Immediate/Next Actions" column on the calendar. This is where the rubber hits the road.

Scheduling these items on the calendar ensures that time is set aside so you don't get caught up with meetings and other activities, but rather have a scheduled time slot applied towards your priorities.

Obviously scheduling is a mechanical process. You sort your list by due date, so that items that are due sooner appear on top. Then you start scheduling the activities on your calendar. Let us demonstrate this process before we dive into some important observations. Let us start with the first row on Mark's Immediate Priorities Matrix™:

Table 12: First priority in the matrix

Priority	Breakdown	Immediate/ Next Actions	Estimated Time	Deadline
Ally technologies	Install new software Plan first session Update Joan & team Send material to printer Train the trainer Schedule final dates	Install new software Ask Joan for dates	60 min 5 min	Wednesday March 21

Mark needs to get the new software installed by Wednesday, and this requires an hour of his time, so he reserves an hour for this task on his calendar on Monday:

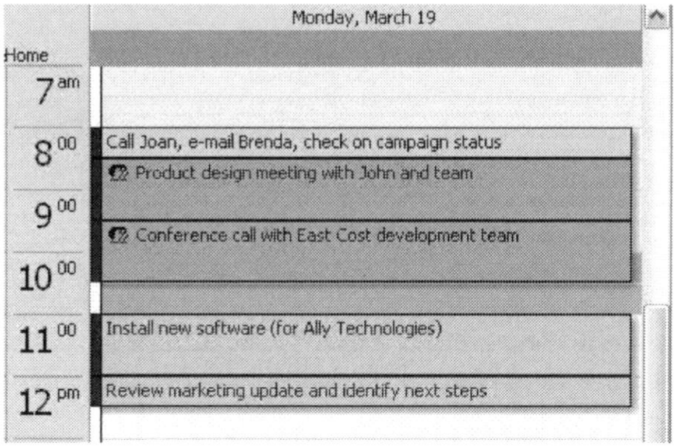

Figure 2: Activity scheduled on the calendar

Then he decides to ask Joan for dates on Tuesday morning, together with a number of other follow-ups that he plans to do that morning:

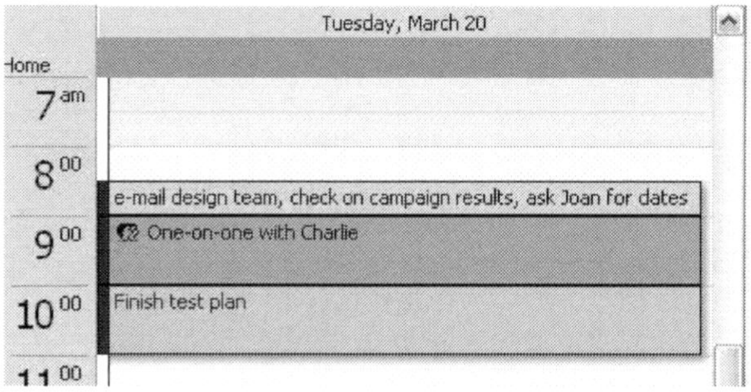

Figure 3: Follow-up scheduled on the calendar

Mark proceeds to schedule the rest of the activities on his Immediate Priorities Matrix™, one activity after another, as described above. In an ideal world he will be able to schedule all the necessary activities within the specified deadlines. However in real life, Mark (and most of us in today's information overload) is likely to "run out of time" and not be able to schedule all the necessary activities. In other words, our calendar is likely to fill up before we are half-way through the matrix. This happened to Mark when he was trying to schedule the budget update:

Table 13: Priority that cannot be scheduled

Budget update	Review latest input Update the sales projections Finalize the new hosted services agreements Send them to Joan for her input	Plan what is needed, and who will be contributing to this process, and delegate accordingly	2 hours	Thu Mar 22

So what should Mark do now? And what should he do with the remaining activities? The answer comes from two important strategies. First is managing expectations. Second is negotiation.

Managing Expectations

Managing expectations starts with informing those who might be impacted by these activities, that they are not going to be completed within the expected timeframes. In the case of the budget update, Mark identifys who is expecting these updates, and who else might be impacted by these updates, and communicates the delay promptly and clearly. Sometimes, this communication is enough and it helps everyone plan their work accordingly. However, sometimes the impact is more significant, and this is where negotiation kicks in.

Negotiation

If delaying the budget update is not acceptable, then Mark needs to put his negotiation hat on, and start to explore ways in which he can help solve this resource conflict. This is where the Immediate Priorities Matrix™ becomes an effective negotiation tool. With the matrix in hand, Mark can point out what other activities are taking up his time and energy, and see if together with the other stakeholders, they can identify areas where he can delay, delegate or adjust scope, in order to make room for the budget update. The Immediate Priorities Matrix™ can turn such negotiation into constructive problem solving sessions where everyone's creativity rises to the occasion and everyone works collaboratively to find a plausible solution. Without the data and objective nature of the Immediate Priorities Matrix™, such discussions can easily get sidetracked and become confrontational and futile.

Keep thinking 80/20

An important concept to keep in mind as we manage expectations and negotiate is the 80/20 rule. Remember that 80% of our results come from 20% of our effort. This can help shed some light on what is truly important, and help make meaningful tradeoffs. One of the activities you have already scheduled on your calendar, can be delayed or cancelled, to make room for another more important activity that is going to yield a much higher return.

But I don't have time

Once in a while, a workshop participant indicates that she already has this information (the information that is supposed to be in the Immediate Priorities Matrix™) in other project documents and therefore questions why she should spend the time to put it in the Immediate Priorities Matrix™, not to mention, there isn't enough time to do so.

The Immediate Priorities Matrix™ is not supposed to replace project management documents or other supporting documents. It is meant to pull the essence of what is going on into one view. It is meant to be succinct (15 or 20 minutes worth of work) and unlike project documents that represent whole projects and whole teams over a period of time, the matrix is a snapshot of what is going on now and up to two weeks from now. Most importantly, it is primarily a rescue tool for those times when you feel overwhelmed. If you are managing well and don't need rescuing from information overload and conflicting demands, then you can just keep it in mind for when you need it. Unless (like many workshop participants opt to do) you decide to use it as a planning tool.

Immediate Priorities Matrix™ as a Planning Tool

Why wait to get overwhelmed and in need of rescuing? Why not prepare the matrix regularly or on an as-needed basis, to help us get *one clear view* of what is going on in our world (not our team, not our company, just us), and what is going on now (not now through the life of the project or budget cycle or whatever else, but only now and up to two weeks from now) and plan these important activities on our calendar. Why not be in charge instead of feeling pulled in all directions? This is what many participants discover as they develop the habit of resorting periodically to the Immediate Priorities Matrix™.

Exercise 1: Immediate Priorities Matrix™

Fill out the matrix below with your priorities as explained in this chapter and then proceed to reserve some time on your calendar for the activities that have important deadlines associated with them.

Table 14: Immediate Priorities Matrix™

Priority	Breakdown	Immediate/ Next Actions	Estimated Time	Deadline

Action Plan

Identify the action items that you would like to take as a result of what was covered in this chapter. Indicate the timeframe in which you plan on taking these actions. Then report on the actual date in which you implemented them and a brief note about the results.

Table 10: Action Plan

Practice/Technique	I will start implementing this on (date?)	Actual start date	Actual end date	Comment/Results
Preparing my Immediate Priorities Matrix™				
Scheduling important activities on my calendar				
Setting expectations and negotiate timelines as necessary				
Add your own item:				
Add your own item:				
Add your own item:				

Chapter 9: The Results You Want – align daily activities with long term goals

In the previous chapter, we discussed the Immediate Priorities Matrix™ as a rescue tool and a planning tool to help us manage conflicting demands, feel less overwhelmed and more in control, manage expectations and negotiate effectively with others. The matrix dealt primarily with the immediate (the now and up to two weeks from now). Now that we have a better handle on the immediate, it is time to turn our attention to the longer term, and make sure that our daily effort is adding up to more significant longer term results. In this chapter, we will be introducing yet another matrix, the End Results Matrix™ which unlike the Immediate Priorities Matrix™ is intended to focus on the next 3 to 6 months.

Defining the End Results

Turn to a new page in the journal and write down today's date, and what you want to accomplish today which is "managing results". Start the Capture Page to capture the myriad of items that come up during the day so they don't interrupt your flow. Then start the Notes pages to capture meeting notes. We are now ready to tackle the topic of conflicting priorities and how we can best manage them.

On the Notes Page, list 3 to 5 key results that you intend to achieve in the next 3 to 6 months. This is what Joan wrote down in her first pass:

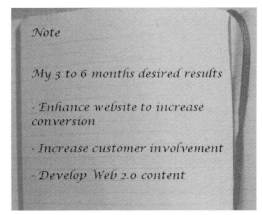

Figure 1: Desired results for next 3 to 6 months

Then as she thought through these results further, she started to be more specific. The more specific, more measurable, and attainable the results are the better. This is what the second pass looked like:

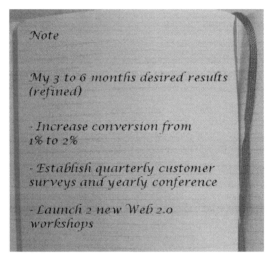

Figure 2: Results clarified

The End Results Matrix™

Once we have clarified the results that we are seeking in the next 3 to 6 months, the next step is to figure out the specific projects and activities that are necessary to create these results. This is the essence of what the End Results Matrix™ is about. Here is the format of the matrix:

Table 15: Sample End Results Matrix™

Result	Projects and tasks	Additional details

This is a sample end result detailed in the matrix:

Table 16: Sample result detailed in the matrix

Increase conversion from 1% to 2%	Enhance usability on website	Review website analytics Identify drop-off points Consult with a usability expert Redesign navigation Fill gaps in content Perform pilot test Implement remaining Web Pages

	Start loyalty program	Brainstorm with team Survey customers Get expert opinion Plan program
	Provide live support	Explore platforms Identify cost effective options Present plan to management

One of the valuable benefits of the End Results Matrix™ is that it prompts us to think through how we are going to get to our end results. It is the catalyst for strategic thinking and to planning the implementation details. These details may need to be further defined in other supporting documents as necessary.

The Immediate Priorities Matrix™ versus the End Results Matrix™

When you complete your End Results Matrix™, take a moment to compare it to your Immediate Priorities Matrix™. Go through the activities you have identified as immediate (and that are occupying your time and energy now and in the next two weeks) and compare them to the activities in the End Results Matrix™ and which are necessary for you to reach your 3 to 6 months results. What do you find when you compare these activities?

Most participants find that these activities do not match. They are out of sync. In other words, the kinds of activities that are keeping us busy on a daily basis, are not the same activities that are necessary for us to reach our long term results. What is the conclusion? Unfortunately, if we continue working this way, we will never reach the results we are hoping for. We end up disappointed, frustrated, and feeling not in control.

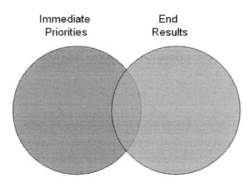

Figure 3: Misalignment between daily priorities and desired results

What we need is to align our daily activities with our long term results. This is probably one of the most crucial undertakings that we can possibly take and the most rewarding one. Here are some ideas on how this can be achieved.

From matrix to calendar again

In the previous chapter, we did the "matrix to calendar" exercise with our Immediate Priorities Matrix™ and it was intended for us to get a better handle on our competing priorities (and better manage expectations and negotiate resources and time when necessary). This time, we will do the "matrix to calendar" exercise for the End Results Matrix™. The goal is to schedule these activities (at least the initial ones that are necessary to get the related projects and initiatives started) on our calendar so they become reality.

The challenge we face most when we try to schedule such activities on our calendar is that our time is already fully scheduled for several weeks. It would be difficult if not impossible to add more activities to our calendar. The trick here is to look beyond the next few weeks and start to put these activities on our calendar for the future—maybe 2, 3, or even 4 weeks from now. Meanwhile, we can start to have informal conversations about these activities, get further buy-in from the stakeholders if necessary, start to work on setting expectations and negotiating resources and scope, and paving the road for success.

In one or two months, as we seriously engage in this alignment process, and bring more of our End Results Matrix™ activities to our calendar (and therefore to reality), our daily priorities are going to be more and more aligned with our end results:

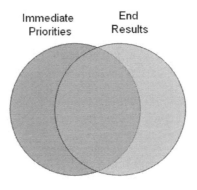

Figure 4: Priorities and results aligned

How often do we go back to these matrices?

As previously discussed, the Immediate Priorities Matrix™ is a tool that you can use on an as-needed basis or periodically such as every two weeks. The End Results Matrix™ on the other hand deals with 3 to 6 month periods and therefore it is likely that you would do it once every 3 to 6 months. The world is very dynamic however, and it continues to change unexpectedly and more frequently that we might desire. With these matrices in hand, we are always ready to respond to the change, and adjust as necessary.

Exercise 1: End Results Matrix™

Fill out the matrix below with your 3 to 5 key end results and the projects/tasks that will help you achieve these end results.

Table 17: End Results Matrix

Result	Projects and tasks	Additional details

Action Plan

Identify the action items that you would like to take as a result of what was covered in this chapter. Indicate the timeframe in which you plan on taking these actions. Then report on the actual date in which you implemented them and a brief note about the results.

Table 2: Action Plan

Practice/Technique	I will start implementing this on (date?)	Actual start date	Actual end date	Comment/Results
Prepare my End Results Matrix™				
Prepare supporting plans and relevant information				
Negotiate and get buy-in				
Schedule important tasks on my calendar				
Add your own item:				
Add your own item:				
Add your own item:				

Chapter 10: The De-stress Secrets—manage stress before it manages you

Turn to a new page in the journal and write down today's date, and what you want to accomplish today which is "manage stress". Start the Capture Page and the Notes page. We are now ready to tackle the topic of managing stress in the workplace. Let us start with this exercise which you can do on the Notes page. Fill in the blank in this sentence:

Stress is when_____

Go ahead, take a few minutes and jot down the various situations that cause you to be stressed. Write down as many as you can.

When we ask our workshop participants to do this exercise, we get items such as:

Stress is…

- when I am asked to do more things than what I have time for
- When priorities keep changing on me
- When my colleagues don't deliver what they promised and therefore I cannot get my tasks completed
- When I am not able to do a great job because of factors that are outside my control
- When I don't know the answer
- When I am held responsible for something I have not done
- When I have difficult people to deal with
- and many more!

I would like to suggest that all of the above situations, and probably the ones that you have written down in your journal, are likely to fall in the following categories:

- ➢ Unfinished/unresolved items lurking in the background
- ➢ People who (or things that) are not the way that we want them to be
- ➢ Being overly concerned about what happened in the past or might happen in the future

In the rest of this chapter, we will explore three primary techniques that can help us better manage the above situations. If you practice these techniques, you are likely to reduce stress significantly. The goal here is not to eliminate stress (which is not desired because some level of stress is healthy and can be quite motivating), but to contain it, manage it well, and get it to work for you instead of against you. As you start to manage stress effectively, the energy that has been taken over by stress will be released and your accomplishments are likely to multiply. Your ability to focus and collaborate will increase dramatically and most importantly, you feed good, or even great, and sometimes ecstatic.

First Technique: The Awareness Wheel

The Awareness Wheel, a technique that was originally described by Sherod & Phyllis Miller (authors of "Core Communication, Skills and Processes") can help us take a difficult situation, break it down into more manageable components and identify how best to handle it. The pre-requisite to using the Awareness Wheel is to clearly define the difficult situation or issue. Clearly defining the situation is an important first step in this process. When the situation is not clearly defined, it is especially difficult to work with. It would be like chasing a ghost.

Then the next step would be to break down this seemingly difficult situation into five components which are presented in the five sections of the wheel below.

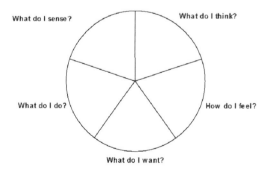

Figure 1: Awareness Wheel

Let us walk through each of these components.

Each component presents a question that you need to answer to the best of your ability. These questions prompt us to think more thoroughly about the situation and identify what is truly going on so we can be in a better position to manage the situation. Below are the questions and what they mean.

1. What do I sense about the situation? We have five senses that give us specific data about the environment we live in. The point here is to identify what this data is such as what did I see and what did I hear.

2. What do I think about the situation? This has to do with what is going on in our mind. And a lot is usually going on in our mind. These range from interpretations, to opinions, to conclusions, and a lot more.

3. How do I feel about the situation? Examples may be sadness, anger, or fear on one side, and joy, and happiness, on the other side, and all shades in between.

4. What do I want in this situation? This has to do with being more aware of our wants, and as we go through the wheel, becoming more aware of our real wants (as opposed to the initial reactionary wants).

5. What do I do in this situation? This has to do with identifying the potential actions and ideally the best possible action.

In a perfect world, we would be able to run through these questions one by one, become more aware of what is really going on, and be in a better position to identify and take the appropriate action. In the real world however, the complexity of the human mind and emotions, and the interdependence between thoughts and feelings, wants and actions, we are likely to go through this multiple times (hence the concept of a wheel) and not necessarily in order. The case study below illustrates how the Awareness Wheel can be applied to help better manage a difficult situation.

The case study

Mark is unhappy at work and when asked to define the problem, here is how he put it: "My boss doesn't care about my professional development and I am really unhappy at work". This situation is very stressful for Mark and is taking up a lot of his energy. His working relationships are impacted, he is not feeling good at work and even outside work, and his performance is suffering. Let us see how the Awareness Wheel can help. We will demonstrate how a coach can help Mark use the Awareness Wheel to manage this situation:

Coach: "Mark, what happened?"

Mark: "She doesn't care"

Where does Mark's statement ("She doesn't care") fall in the Awareness Wheel? This is Mark's subjective view of what happened. This is clearly his interpretation of what happened. It is a thought. The coach makes a note of this in the Awareness Wheel, indicating to Mark that this is his interpretation, and repeats the question again:

Coach: "Tell me more about what actually happened?"

Mark: "She cancelled the meeting"

This is a fact. Mark reports real data. He *saw* (with his "senses") the meeting cancelled notice in his e-mail inbox. The coach takes note of this and proceeds to help Mark explore the feeling part:

Coach: "Mark, how do you feel about the meeting being cancelled?"

Mark: "I feel I am not important"

Even though Mark uses the words "I feel," the statement "I am not important" is more of an interpretation than a feeling. Using words such as "I feel" to express a thought is common. There might be a feeling associated with the thought, but that is something that would need to be explored. For now, the "I am not important" statement is noted as a thought. Now the coach tries to get to the feeling behind the thought.

Coach: "Mark, how else are you feeling about this?"

Mark pauses for a bit and then says: "I am sad and disappointed"

As you may have noticed already, the coach tends to repeat the same question more than once. The first time, he usually gets a reactionary answer such as "I feel that I am not important" and then the second time (or sometime third or fourth time) he gets more meaningful insights into what is really going on such as "I am sad and disappointed".

The coach continues to explore this area with Mark, and then when he thinks that Mark is ready to move to the next component, the coach makes an initial attempt at asking Mark about his wants.

Coach: "So what do you want Mark"

Mark: "I want to have the meeting"

Then Mark proceeds to say:

Mark: "I will tell her that I am unhappy".

Mark has just expressed an action here (not necessary the best action, but it is an action). The Coach notices that the want and action expressed by Mark are reactionary, so he asks Mark again about his thoughts and feelings about the situation, and gives him the opportunity to express these further and spend time exploring these. Then later in the conversation, the coach makes another attempt at asking Mark about what Mark really wants. Mark takes a deep breath at that point, and says:

Mark: "I want more recognition".

Then Mark adds: "I want input on my career development".

This is a big "Ah-Ha" moment for Mark! Mark just realized it is not the meeting that really got him emotionally mixed up and stressed, it is the underlying need to have recognition and the desire for a better career development plan that he seems to be missing at work. The meeting was just the tip of the iceberg and his reaction to the meeting being cancelled is just that, a reaction. This is one of the key purposes of the wheel – to facilitate the process of becoming more aware of the real causes behind what we are experiencing on the surface.

Occasionally, workshop participants indicate that Mark should have easily realized that it was not the meeting that was causing his stress ("what is the big deal about a meeting being cancelled anyway"), and that it should have been clear to him that the lack of recognition and lack of career development opportunities were the real issues. When we talk to these participants further about the issues that are causing "them" stress, we find out that their issues are not more severe or different in nature from Mark's issues, and yet, these participants seem to get significantly stressed and emotionally involved when it comes to their own issues. So how does it happen that we have more clarity when it comes to other people's issues, and suddenly lose this clarity when it comes to our own issues?

This is largely because when we are experiencing the issues ourselves, we are "under their influence", emotionally involved in them, and therefore our judgment gets impaired. Yes indeed. Our Judgment gets impaired. At this point, when it gets impaired, even the smartest of us become unable (truly unable) to make the slightest distinction between data, opinions, feelings, and wants. Our emotions and deep seated fears take over. So while Mark's situation may seem easy to someone looking at it from the outside, maybe someone who hasn't experienced a similar situation, it doesn't look that way for Mark, and probably for anyone who has experienced a similar situation.

In order to truly experience the Awareness Wheel, better understand it and see its usefulness, you need to apply it to a real situation that is causing you significant stress, substantial confusion, and inability to manage the situation effectively – a situation where your judgment is impaired. If you cannot think of such a situation, the Awareness Wheel and underlying concepts are likely to be helpful in better understanding and dealing with others who are experiencing these situations.

Back to Mark, the coach is now ready to ask the important question:

Coach: "So what are you going to do about this situation Mark?"

Mark: "I will ask to reschedule the meeting and discuss the real issues with my boss"

Then Mark adds: "I will also find a coach or a mentor"

Another big "Ah-Ha"!

The Awareness Wheel helped transform this difficult situation (or even seemingly insurmountable situation in Mark's mind at the time when his judgment is impaired) into an actionable one. We started with "My boss doesn't care about my professional development and I am really unhappy at work" and ended up with a better understanding of the underlying needs and specific action items that can be carried out in order to get these underlying needs met. Nicely done!

The job is not done however. Mark still needs to implement these actions. As he implements the actions, he needs to watch for his interpretations and assumptions sneaking in again. If he continues practicing the Awareness Wheel each step of the way, he will continue to refine and enhance his actions. Soon he will become experienced at this tool and use it more naturally to help him through difficult situations. He is now on his way to discovering a whole new world of accomplishments.

The purpose of the wheel

To start with, the simple act of defining the "issue" and getting engaged with the Awareness Wheel is in and by itself an empowering exercise. It puts our energy and creativity in motion. It helps us challenge the status quo and get busy with solutions – all essential to solving problems and feeling better. In addition, the Awareness Wheel serves several important and clear purposes:

1. It help us separate reality from imagination (events from interpretations)

2. It help us separate thoughts from feelings (what the mind is creating, as opposed to how we are truly feeling)

3. It help us identify our true wants (instead of our reactionary wants)

4. It facilitates identifying the best possible action

5. It enables us to positively influence our end results

In our daily work and personal life, the default sequence of events is that an event takes place in our environment for instance. we sense something (someone says or does something), we quickly interpret it in a certain way (unfortunately this may be the not-so-constructive way), we feel a certain way about it (not so positive feelings caused by not-so-constructive interpretations), and then act accordingly (poor action caused by this sequence). This whole sequence happens very quickly and transparently. We don't even notice it. It looks and feels as if we are just taking actions to deal with what happened, yet we wonder why we aren't getting the results we desire. The Awareness Wheel enables us to interfere and change this sequence. The end goal is significantly improved actions and results, not to mention breakthroughs!

Exhaust your creative thinking and problem solving skills

While there are certain difficult situations that we cannot do anything about, more often than not, it is possible to come up with plausible actions that we can take. This is exactly where creative thinking and problem solving come into play. This is where we want to go beyond the obvious, do our research, brainstorm with others, and uncover new possibilities.

It is difficult to get to the creative thinking and problem solving stage if we are stuck in our biased interpretations, negative feelings, and rigid wants. The Awareness Wheel can help us release these interpretations, feelings, and wants, and therefore go beyond them and apply our time and energy into formulating constructive actions.

So what if there is nothing we can do about the situation?

What if we go through the Awareness Wheel, exhaust our creative thinking and problem solving capabilities, and still conclude that there isn't much that we can do about the situation. If this is the case, it would be beneficial for us to stop banging our head against this situation and move on to better things – where our effort is fruitful and rewarding. The Awareness Wheel helps us make that determination faster and reach the acceptance stage sooner. Once we reach the acceptance stage, I would even suggest creating a "closed issues" category in the catch-all to-do list and adding the issue to that category so that our mind doesn't keep resurrecting the "closed" issue and wasting valuable energy.

Self-Coaching

We presented the case study above by having a coach walk through the Awareness Wheel with Mark. While it would be ideal to have a coach help us along the way, more often than not, we need to be our own coach. The Awareness Wheel is the ideal tool for self-coaching.

The Awareness Wheel components and related questions are exactly the kind of questions we should ask ourselves. Writing down the answers, as we progress through the process, is critical. This helps us avoid "spinning our wheels" by reiterating the same thoughts and feelings endlessly. This will also help us detect "imbalance" (spending too much time and energy on one component of the wheel without paying enough attention to the rest). The Awareness Wheel is largely about balance. It helps bring to the forefront all aspects of a situation. It helps us have a more objective view of the world as opposed to getting too focused on one area and losing ourselves in it.

As we saw in the case study, it is important to repeat the same question more than once to get beyond the initial superficial answer. It usually takes several passes to get to the core issues. If you don't get to the desired results in one session, you may want to give yourself a break, let the issues percolate, and then resume later. This process of self-questioning and self-coaching is one of the most worthwhile activities we can undertake if we want to succeed and feel better – accomplish more with less stress.

Coaching each other

Be careful! When it comes to coaching others to use the Awareness Wheel, things can get tricky. It is most tricky if you are in the midst of a conflict situation or a heated discussion with the other person. It is tempting at that time to want to share the Awareness Wheel techniques with the other party to help solve the situation. Your good intentions may not generate the desired results because the other party may not be open to coaching especially not in this setting.

However if you have already built some trust with the other party and shared the Awareness Wheel techniques ahead of time, and both agree that it would be beneficial to help each other through it when necessary, things can be much more promising.

And in situations where it is not possible or appropriate to share the Awareness Wheel and coach each other, one can still keep the Awareness Wheel handy and apply the techniques to help the situation. Using the Awareness Wheel should not depend on the other party and does not need to be a formal exercise. It can help us better understand what is going on for us, and potentially for the other party, and have a more effective interaction as a result.

For instance, it is far more empowering and effective to say "I saw that you cancelled this meeting" (the senses) and "my interpretation was that this issue is not important to you right now" (the thought), and "I felt nervous" (feeling), and then continue to say "I would like to make sure we move this issue forward and not run into potential project delays later" (want), and "what do you think we can do to address this situation?" (request for action in the form of a question). This is common sense and mature communication that can be achieved by practicing the Awareness Wheel and applying it genuinely to everyday situations.

Second Technique: Rational Thinking

The Rational Emotive Theory which was pioneered by Dr. Albert Ellis, the author of "How to stubbornly refuse to make yourself miserable about anything – yes anything" has some valuable insights to offer when it comes to managing stress.

When we are overly stressed about a situation, it is very likely that we have an irrational (unrealistic) believe about the situation that is causing the extra stress, more so than the situation itself. This is common sense and commonly forgotten. The situation itself may call for some caution, and may be uncomfortable, or even stressful, but it is the underlying belief that is likely to be causing the "overly" stressful perception and the thoughts and feelings that "we cannot stand it".

If we uncover this underlying irrational belief, and work at replacing it with a more rational (realistic) belief, then it is likely that at the minimum we will be a lot less stressed, and at best, we may even be in a position to take more constructive actions and influence the situation positively.

The case study

Mark is overly stressed and almost panicky when John doesn't turn in his status report on time. Mark cannot stand the situation, he's angry, and he cannot stand John when this happens. This is affecting his working relationship with John and his ability to come up with a workable solution for this issue. This is also affecting his feeling about his work, his team, and the whole organization that allows someone like John to get away with this behavior.

What is the underlying irrational belief(s) behind Mark's problem? We can probably identify several of them – depending on how deep we want to go with our analysis. However, for the sake of our case study, let us stick to these two:

1. People "should" give their status reports on time

2. "I cannot stand it" when they don't give their status report on time

Well, let us examine these beliefs further. They are both unrealistic. They don't conform to reality. Beliefs that don't conform to reality are likely to bring us frustration and stress. The first belief includes a strong "should". Whenever we hold on to beliefs that are loaded with strong "shoulds", we are asking for trouble. Who said or guaranteed us that people "should" give their status reports on time? No one ever did. This belief is not real. The proof that this belief is not real is that people aren't giving their status reports on time. If it was such a given that people "should" give their status report on time, then they would. But in reality some of them don't, and therefore this "should" is unrealistic. The second belief includes another unrealistic statement: "I cannot stand it when____". In reality Mark is standing it. He hasn't vanished and life is still going on.

So what would be the more rational beliefs that could replace the irrational ones mentioned above? How about: "It is frustrating when John doesn't give his status report on time, however even though it is inconvenient and not ideal, I can stand it and I can manage it". This is reality!

Working at replacing initial beliefs that are rigid and unrealistic with the second one, which is flexible and realistic, is likely to cause the following:

1. Mark will feel better. By simply thinking about the situation differently, he is going to feel less stressed about it.

2. With the new attitude, Mark is likely to be in a better position to have a more constructive conversation with John and potentially better understand the underlying reasons for the situation and come up with some workable solutions.

Easier said than done

Mark may go through the above exercise and identify the irrational belief and then the more constructive rational belief. However when it comes down to it, he may still feel that he cannot stand it and have the same resentment towards John which prevents him from feeling better and having a more constructive conversation.

Beliefs run deep. They have an amazing power over us. So how do we release the strong hold they have over us? How do we "enable" more rational beliefs that we identify? These are some techniques that can help:

a) Disputing them over and over again.

b) Acting against them over and over again.

Disputing them over and over can loosen them up. It is like taking their mask away so we can see them for what they truly are; unrealistic or exaggerated views of the world. Usually this is an important first step before we take action. Acting against our irrational beliefs is by far the most effective way to transform our learning from being emotional and momentary to being intellectual and lasting.

How Rational Thinking complements the Awareness Wheel

Rational thinking can also help us dispute those interpretations, assumptions, and opinions that are unrealistic and therefore cause us a great deal of stress. In Mark's case, he interpreted his boss's cancellation of the meeting as "she doesn't care about my professional development". This is irrational and unrealistic. Cancelling the meeting doesn't prove that his boss doesn't care. Mark might change this to "my interpretation is that she doesn't care" or "it is possible that she doesn't care, and it is possible that there are other reasons which I should explore". These are more realistic interpretations and they can help Mark explore other aspects of the wheel instead of being stuck in this interpretation.

Rational thinking can also help us replace rigid and unrealistic wants by softer and more realistic versions. So instead of holding on to "I want her to reschedule the meeting", it would be more realistic to change this to "I would like to reschedule the meeting, but if she doesn't, I can stand it and I can manage", and then move on to figuring out the best possible action.

When we go through the wheel and conclude that there isn't much that we can do about a situation, then rational thinking can help us accept the situation and let go of our childish belief that the situation "should" be different. Instead of holding on to the belief that "it should be different", we can replace it by a more realistic version which might acknowledge that "it would be nice if it was different, but even though it is the way it is, and it is inconvenient and undesirable, I can stand it and manage through it".

Third Technique: Being in the Present

If we are not in the "present", meaning not fully aware of what is going on right now, how can we make good decisions and have a positive impact on the future? Being in the present and noticing what is going on around us are pre-requisites for making better plans and better choices for the future. Not to mention that when we are in the present, we are likely to be more in touch with reality and not as subjected to irrational beliefs that can cause unnecessary stress. We are also likely to be more

---

connected with the people around us and build better working relationships. All are ingredients for accomplishing a lot more with a lot less stress.

The past and the future are the making of our mind

It is easy to see how the future is the making of our mind. After all it hasn't happened yet. It is a projection that our mind creates about what it thinks will happen at some point in time. But how would you explain how the past is the making of our mind? That is because the "past" is what we remember from the past and not necessarily what actually happened in the past. Our memory unfortunately tends to be quite selective. Take a look at the Awareness Wheel again. When we remember a past situation, which parts of the Awareness Wheel do you think we are likely to remember?

It is more likely that we remember our interpretations, opinions, some of the feelings we experienced, and if we haven't identified our true wants at that time, we are likely to remember our superficial wants and whatever uninformed action we may have taken at the time. If Mark hadn't gone through the Awareness Wheel, he would have remembered that his boss "didn't care about his professional development and that he was really unhappy at work", and may have even drawn some additional irrational conclusions such as "bosses don't care" and "the workplace is really difficult and unfair".

If the past and the future are largely the making of our mind, doesn't it make sense to focus our energy on the present, and be more fully prepared to take better actions towards the future (instead of dwelling about the past or worrying about the future)?

Use the Awareness Wheel to be in the present

If you are still holding on to an event that happened in the past, find yourself preoccupied with it, and even stressed about it, the Awareness Wheel can help. Even if there is nothing that you can do about the event anymore, going through the wheel helps you shed some light on what really happened. You may be able to identify what your real wants were at the time, and what options you might have had. This can transform this past event from being an unpleasant or even daunting one to being a lesson learned. You can also "close" this issue and add it to the "closed issues" category in the catch-all to-do list.

As you can see the Awareness Wheel is multi-dimensional. It can be applied to current events that we need to address now. It can be applied to past events that are still unresolved in our mind. We can even apply it to potential future events that we are concerned about to feel better about them now and be proactive in preparing for them.

Exercise 1: Issues that are causing stress

Use this table to list the issues that are causing you stress and identify which of the above techniques is likely to help. Then after you apply the technique on each issue (using the diagrams detailed below), write down your comments and a brief description of the results.

Table 1: Issues that are causing stress

Issue	Techniques that is likely to help	Comment/Results

Exercise 2: Awareness Wheel

Issue: _____

_____

_____

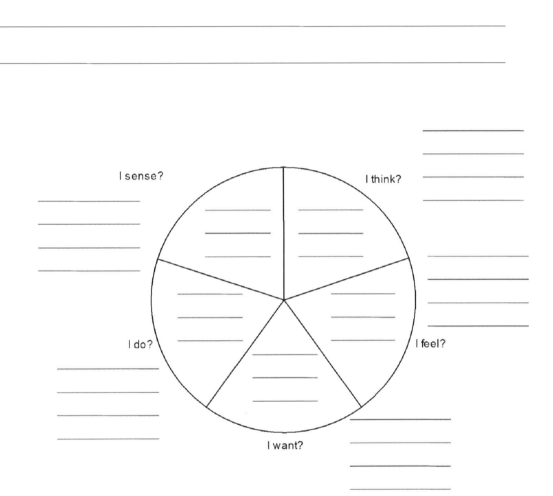

Exercise 3: Rational Thinking Diagram

Issue: _____

_____

_____

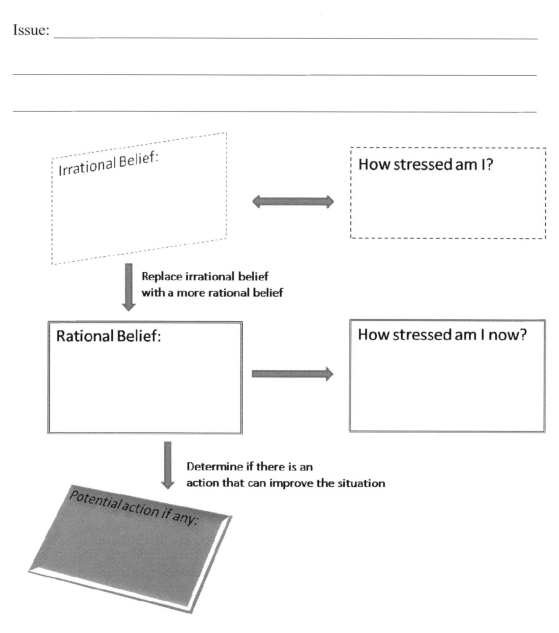

Action Plan

Identify the action items that you would like to take as a result of what was covered in this chapter. Indicate the timeframe in which you plan on taking these actions. Then report on the actual date in which you implemented them and a brief note about the results.

Table 2: Action Plan

Practice/Technique	I will start implementing this on (date?)	Actual start date	Actual end date	Comment/Results
Identify the issues that are causing you considerable stress				
Use the Awareness Wheel and/or the Rational Thinking Diagram to identify potential solutions				
Add your own item:				
Add your own item:				
Add your own item:				

Chapter 11: Use collaboration technologies to accelerate everything

Individual productivity is highly intertwined with group productivity. Our ability to share information and collaborate with others largely determines how much we accomplish as individuals, as groups, and as organizations. Furthermore, teams are becoming increasingly more virtual and workers are becoming increasingly more mobile.

In this chapter, we will explore some key technologies that can help us collaborate more effectively with others, reduce our over-dependence on e-mail and meetings, and be more productive when we are working on virtual teams or on-the-go. This is not a side issue to the "Accomplishing more in less time, less effort, and less stress" arena. This is a core issue that addresses root causes behind why we don't get enough accomplished and feel overwhelmed with information.

Blogs

If you or someone in your team or organization has important knowledge that others need, or has an audience to engage, it is imperative to start a blog if you haven't already. Blogs can be a powerful communication tool that can help individuals, teams, and organizations transform how they share knowledge, promote products, provide services, advance ideas, and influence audience behaviors.

Starting with the basics

A blog is a user-generated website where entries are displayed in reverse chronological order. Blogs adhere closely to the "most recent on top" concept we introduced earlier in the book. Blogs provide commentary or news on a particular subject. They can be personal or business and they can be private or public as illustrated in the diagram below. In the "Accomplishing more with less" context, we are mostly interested in the lower right quadrant:

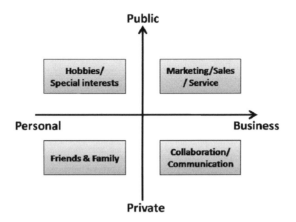

Figure 1: Types of blogs

This "most recent on top" approach makes a blog ideal for telling a story, or building knowledge over time as new pieces of information become available. Blogs also adhere to the "as-needed basis" concept which we referred to previously. New information is added if/when necessary.

Blogging platforms also provide traditional website functionality such as the ability to include static web pages. This means in addition to the developing a story or knowledge, you can easily include information about the company, the team, the products and services, and whatever else is necessary to support the purpose of the blog.

Anatomy of a blog

Let us explore the key parts that make up a blog using the less-is-more blog which is one of the blogs that we publish (less-is-more.typepad.com).

First part: The identity

The identity consists of the URL of the blog, the title, the tag line, and the about page. Identity is important. It needs to quickly tell the visitor what the blog is about and how it benefits them. If the identity is not clear or the value proposition not compelling, the reader is likely to move on to the next thing.

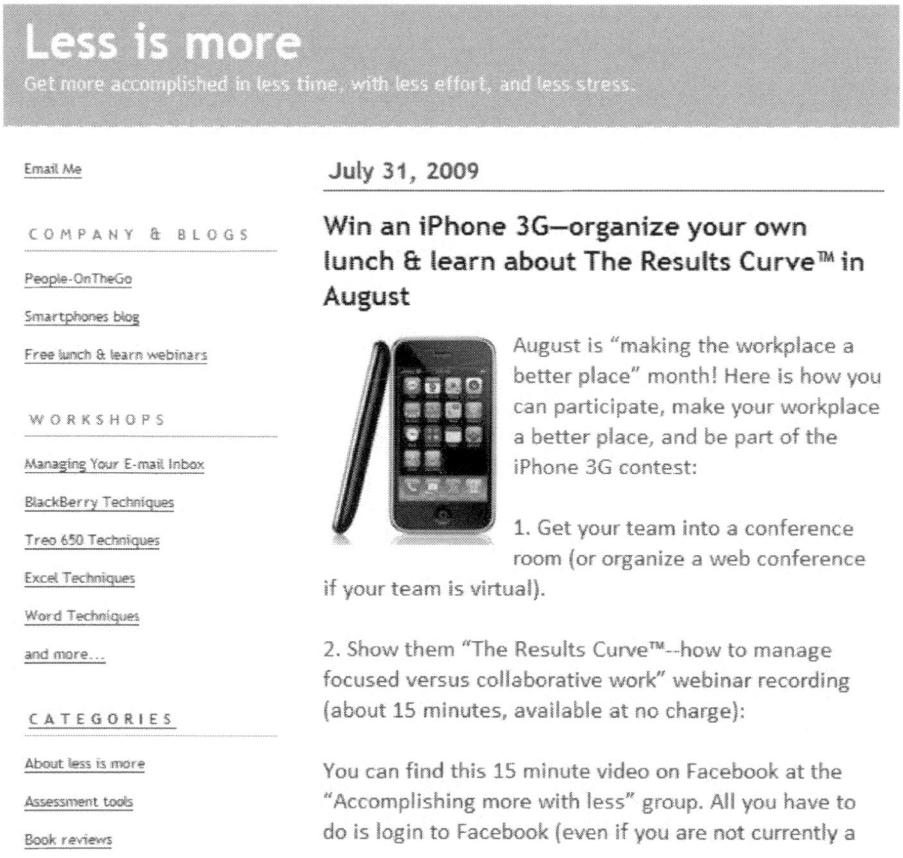

Less is more
Get more accomplished in less time, with less effort, and less stress.

Email Me

COMPANY & BLOGS

People-OnTheGo

Smartphones blog

Free lunch & learn webinars

WORKSHOPS

Managing Your E-mail Inbox

BlackBerry Techniques

Treo 650 Techniques

Excel Techniques

Word Techniques

and more...

CATEGORIES

About less is more

Assessment tools

Book reviews

July 31, 2009

Win an iPhone 3G—organize your own lunch & learn about The Results Curve™ in August

August is "making the workplace a better place" month! Here is how you can participate, make your workplace a better place, and be part of the iPhone 3G contest:

1. Get your team into a conference room (or organize a web conference if your team is virtual).

2. Show them "The Results Curve™--how to manage focused versus collaborative work" webinar recording (about 15 minutes, available at no charge):

You can find this 15 minute video on Facebook at the "Accomplishing more with less" group. All you have to do is login to Facebook (even if you are not currently a

Figure 2: Blog identify (name, tagline, about link)

Second part: The post

The post has a date, a title, and the actual content. The date is quite relevant here. The post you see when you visit the main page is the most recent.

The content includes text, images, and links to other posts in the same blog, or to other blogs and websites, as well as to audio files, video files, and documents of various formats. A post is usually focused on a specific topic and tends to be short and to the point.

It is common for the author of a post to categorize the post by assigning one or more categories. The categories, which are basically topics, are then displayed as a navigational menu usually on the side of the blog home page. This makes it easy for the reader to quickly find posts that relate to a certain topic.

Other blogs and website can link to each blog post individually using what is called a "Permalink". The Permalink remains the same even if the post is modified.

Third part: The comments

Comments make a blog a two way conversation. Readers can easily add their comments as well as read other readers' comments. Comments can be about the original post or about other comments. This makes blogs very engaging and an effective platform for getting feedback and conducting research.

Fourth part: The subscription

Blogs allow us to subscribe to them using an RSS reader such as Google Reader and My Yahoo. The RSS reader tracks all new posts that get posted and that haven't been read yet. This enables us to see at a glance a list of the unread posts in the blogs that we subscribe to, and easily read the desired ones. This makes staying up to date with our favorite blogs easy and efficient.

Behind the scene

This is a sample screen where an author of a blog composes and publishes a blog post:

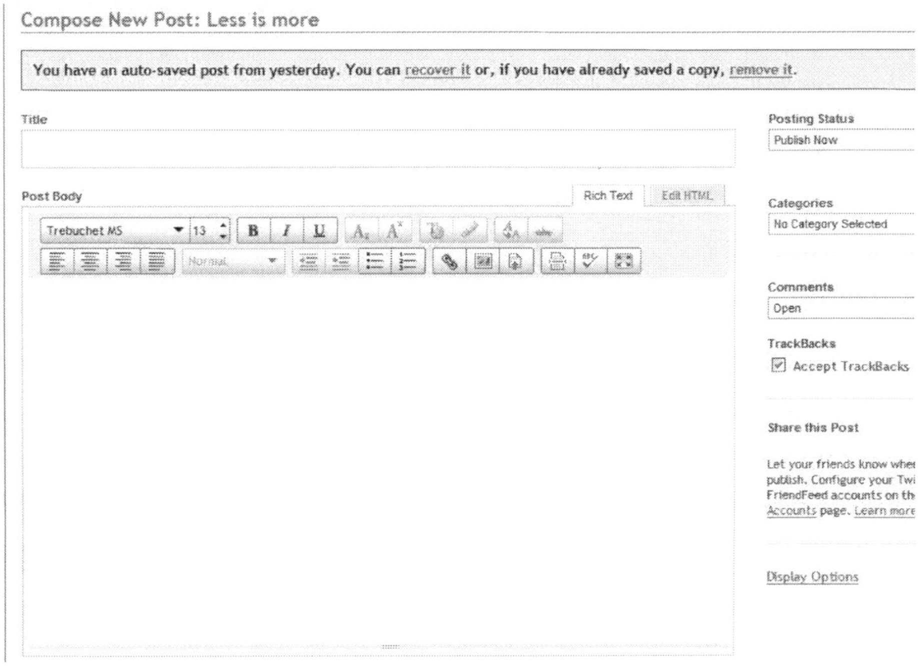

Figure 3: Blog post composition similar to e-mail composition

What does this screen look like? This looks like an e-mail composition screen. Writing a blog post is not much different from writing an e-mail. If you are a subject matter expert on your team, and you get a question from a team member, how do you currently answer it? Most people answer it via e-mail. As a result, this valuable knowledge is scattered and hidden in mailboxes throughout the organization. This knowledge is difficult to find and next to impossible to leverage. Next time we get a similar question, we end up duplicating our effort, and burying yet another piece of knowledge, never to be seen again.

The amount of effort that is wasted as a result and the opportunity costs are enormous. E-mail is not the right tool for sharing knowledge. If we answer the question in a blog post instead of an e-mail, which is just as easy, and send the sender the link to the blog post (the Permalink mentioned earlier), we can re-use the knowledge later (efficiency) and anyone can access it when they need to and build on it (opportunity). Furthermore, we can keep building on this knowledge, by adding new insights and information to the blog.

The purpose of a blog

Blogs can be very tactical and used to share information about news and events, or more strategic and used to share important knowledge and engage internal and external audiences in mission critical activities. The purposes of a blog can be summarized as follows (in increasing order from very tactical to very strategic):

1. Inform: Provide information about a certain topic

2. Educate: Impart knowledge over time related to an important topic or business activity

3. Engage: Elicit conversations, collect feedback, conduct qualitative market research

4. Motivate: Promote certain actions

5. Impact culture: Promote values and behaviors consistently over time

---

When starting a blog, it is critical to clearly define the blog audience, its purpose, how it will serve this purpose, and specifically what benefits it will bring to its audience. This is a sample template for defining a blog:

Table 18: Defining a blog

Blog title	less-is-more
Blog tagline	Get more accomplished in less time, less effort, and less stress
Blog audience	Business professionals who want to accomplish more and feel more fulfilled
Blog purpose (authors' perspective)	1. Promote and evangelize productivity in the workplace. 2. Create a community of people who are interested in productivity. 3. Engage readers with our activities and training programs.
Specific benefits (reader's perspective)	1. Get answers to frequently asked questions about the subject matter. 2. Get updates about related events. 3. Get supporting material for events and training programs. 4. Learn about new concept and techniques related to productivity. 5. Connect with the authors and other users who have similar interests

Such a definition provides the blog author(s) with clear guidelines on which topics belong to the blog and which don't, and helps keep the blog on track over time.

One special application for blogs relates to customer facing activities. People in the organization who deal directly with external audiences (audiences such as prospects, customers, and partners) can use blogs to portray their daily experiences and insights to internal audiences. This ensures that these experiences are better leveraged when designing or enhancing products and services.

Starting a blog, a three step process

The process consists of the following three steps:

1. Defining the audience, purpose, and benefits.

2. Deciding on a blogging platform

3. Creating the blog

If this is a team blog, the definition of the audience, purpose, and benefits needs to include a team discussion, and an agreement on the related issues. It also needs to involve defining the related processes. The template presented in the previous section, or a variation thereof, could be useful in this step.

Blogging Platforms

If you are within a company, you may already have a blogging platform available to you. If not, you would need to explore the various platforms that are available and determine which fits your needs best. Here are three of the most popular platforms:

Table 19: Popular blogging platforms

Platform	Cost	Hosted?	Enterprise?
Typepad	$4.95-$24.95/month	Yes	Yes
Wordpress	Free (extra features cost $)	Yes	Open Source
Blogger	Free	Yes	Not available

One of the main decisions is whether to use a hosted platform or an enterprise one. A hosted platform resides on the service provider's servers. On one hand, this is an advantage because it requires little setup and virtually no maintenance on your part. On the other hand, some companies have strict policies relating to network security and data management and may prohibit the use of such hosted platforms.

Wikis

A wiki is a website that anyone can edit. Just like blogs, wikis can be public or private, and personal or business. It is not very common to have a personal wiki though. In the "Accomplishing more with less" context, we are mostly interested in internal wikis (private) which are used as a business collaboration tool (business).

Anatomy of a wiki

First part: The identity

While not as critical as it is with blogs, especially when it comes to internal wikis, having a clearly defined identity that includes the purpose and benefits is still important. Companies end up having a long list of internal wikis, and without a clear identity, your wiki can get lost in the shuffle and your effort not well leveraged.

Second part: The edit and save capabilities

These are what make a wiki a "wiki". Editing a page allows the user to add, edit, or delete content. Saving the page applies the changes so they are visible to anyone who visits the page after that.

Most wikis track all changes to a page. Previous versions of the pages are kept so that a user can refer back to them. This makes it easy to retrieve content that has been deleted or modified. Wikis require users to register before they can edit pages, and when a user edits a page, the user information is also tracked. This keeps users honest and professional in their updates.

When two users try to edit the same page, the user who gets there second is notified that this page is being edited. It is typically recommended that the second user waits until the first user is finished editing. However, the second user can choose to still edit the page and have the changes merged with the first user's changes.

Third part: The link capability

Links, just like a hyperlink on a webpage, allow the user to create new pages, also called topics. The user starts by typing the text and highlighting it and then indicating that it is intended to be a link to a new page. When the user saves this page, the text becomes a hyperlink, which can then be clicked to create the new page. The new page is initially blank until the user starts adding content to it and saves it.

The link capability makes it possible to expand the wiki several levels deep just like a typical website. This is an important distinction between wikis and blogs. A blog is one long page with no levels. This is also why wikis can sometimes grow out-of-control and become difficult to manage. Having a good structure to start with and keeping the structure evolving is crucial.

The structure and lifecycle of a wiki

Teams who discuss the structure of their wiki and agree on a "blueprint" for the structure, and evolve and adapt it over time based on the needs of their users, are much more likely to be successful and reap the benefits. Teams that don't are more likely to end up with wikis that are difficult to use and manage.

Some teams choose to have one or more people designated as administrators whose role is to evolve the structure and make sure that the content is aligned with the purpose of the wiki. Others make this a shared responsibility among the wiki contributors. The latter approach is more consistent with the philosophy of wikis. In either case, having guidelines and etiquette that are well documented in the wiki and that continue to evolve over time is highly beneficial.

Wikis are not meant to be used for anything and everything and forever. They are ideal for evolving content and managing and coordinating projects, when new projects and initiative are developing and when collaboration is key. Sometimes when certain milestones are reached, or in future stages of the project, a snapshot of the content can then be leveraged in other formats such as published documents, audio and video files, podcasts, and the like. The wiki may or may not continue to be useful at that point, or in some cases the original wiki may be frozen, and a new wiki or a section with the newly extracted knowledge can be started.

Wikis versus blogs

As we saw earlier, blogs are excellent tools for sharing information, sharing knowledge, engaging audiences, and promoting certain actions and behaviors among other things. Blog posts are written by one or more authors who tend to be the knowledge experts or evangelists of the underlying topic(s). Readers can add their comments to existing posts but cannot write new posts. This makes a blog more of a communication platform. Wikis on the other hand allow all users to add, edit, and delete content, and therefore put everyone involved on an equal footing. This makes wikis more of a collaboration platform. Peter Toney, creator of Twiki.org and Twiki.net (which is one of the most popular enterprise wiki platforms) put it this way: "A blog is the voice of the few while a wiki is the voice of the many".

Starting a wiki, a four step process

Just like starting a blog, starting a wiki involves several steps which start with the definition of the wiki purpose:

1. Defining the audience, purpose, and benefits.

2. Defining the structure and process

3. Deciding on a platform

4. Creating the wiki

As illustrated above, there is one additional step involved in creating a wiki. This relates to the definition of the structure and the process. As mentioned above, wiki users who don't pay enough attention to this area end up creating wikis that are difficult to use and manage that may not serve their purpose well. In addition, some team buy-in and team agreements need to be reached to make the wiki effort sustainable and fruitful.

Wiki Platforms

Here are some of the popular wiki platforms:

Table 20: Popular Wiki Platforms

Platforms	Cost	Hosted	Enterprise
PBWiki	$50 to $250 per month* Up to 75 users	Yes	---
Central Desktop	$25 to $250 per month Up to 100 users	Yes	---
Social Text	Free up to 5 users, then contact sales	Yes	Yes
Confluence	$49 to $249/month Up to 100 users	Yes	Yes
TWiki	Free, additional services ($) available from TWiki.Net	No	Yes

Like blogs, wikis can be hosted at third party service providers or can be installed on the company's servers within the firewall. For those interested in learning more about wiki platforms, wikimatrix.org is a great source of information that includes in-depth comparisons of platforms.

Microsoft SharePoint

Microsoft SharePoint is an add-on to Windows Server which enables the creation of team and project intranets, the sharing and management of documents, calendars, and tasks among other things. It is a powerful collaboration tool as well as an application development platform. There is more to Microsoft SharePoint, but in the AML context, we will focus on the above features.

Document management in SharePoint

SharePoint allows users to create document libraries where documents can be stored and managed. Document libraries are similar in a way to shared network drives. However they are much more capable and are designed to facilitate the collaboration process. They enable multiple users to seamlessly access these documents, track revisions, and manage alerts when documents are updated.

Let us consider this marketing team intranet site in SharePoint and the document library "Collaterals" which was created to help the marketing team collaborate on creating and distributing marketing collaterals:

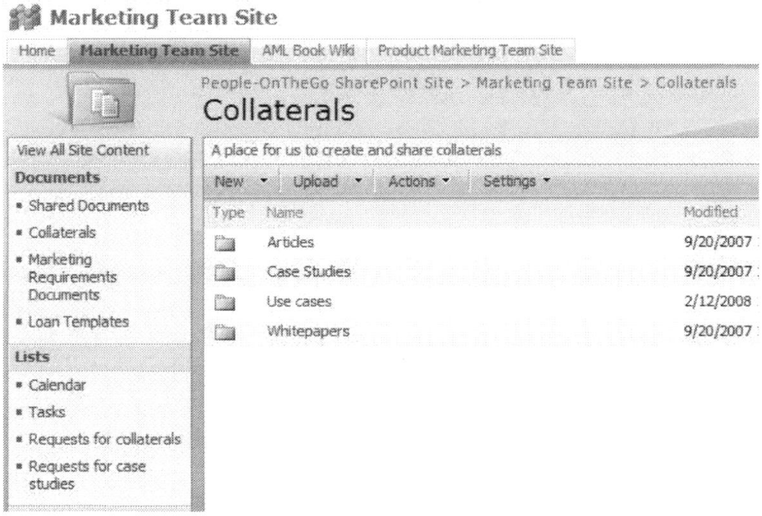

Figure 4: The Collaterals document library folders

Let us consider an article that the marketing team is working on. This article is now loaded into the document library and the marketing team members can easily review it, edit it, and take it to completion. They can also provide the sales team access to the document library so they can see the progress, potentially provide input, and later access the document and use it in their sales effort – all seamlessly and all without e-mail.

A user can open the document for read only or for editing. When a user opens the document for editing, if another user tries to open the document for editing at the same time, SharePoint will display the following notification:

Figure 5: When another user tries to edit the same document

If the second user decides to wait until the document becomes available, once available, SharePoint will display the following notification and allows the user to start editing the document:

Figure 6: When the second user chooses to receive notification

If a user wants to make extensive changes to a document which might take several hours or several days to complete without necessarily being connected to the SharePoint site, SharePoint allows the user to check-out the document, download a copy to the local drive, and then when finished editing the document, check-in the updated document back to SharePoint. During this time when the user has the document checked-out, other users can still access the document as a read-only document.

If revision tracking is enabled on this document library, every time a user makes a change to a document, a new revision is created. Users can view previous revisions, compare them, and if necessary restore a previous revision so it becomes the current revision again. Here is the view that shows the revisions for a document:

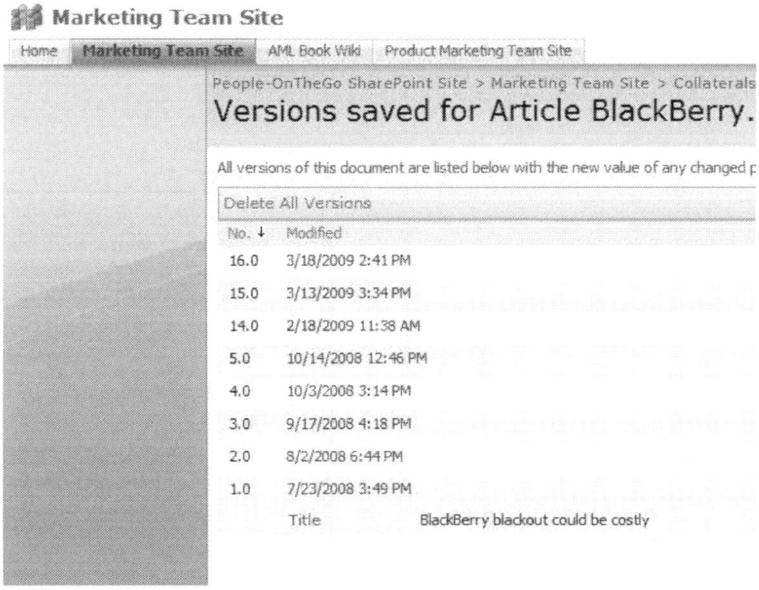

Figure 7: Document version history

Managing documents via e-mail versus in SharePoint

Let us say a team of 5 people is working on a document and they go through 10 revisions before they complete the document. This process, when done via e-mail which is often the case, can be quite inefficient and error prone. This is likely to result in at least 50 copies of the document, but more likely hundreds of copies, scattered in the users' mailboxes. This can also lead to on-going confusion about which is the most recent copy, and whose feedback has been incorporated and whose has not.

If this team uses a document library in SharePoint to manage this process, it will eliminate confusion, make sure all changes are well tracked, and everyone can look at the latest most up-to-date copy of the document. This will cut down on hundreds of e-mails and minimize the storage needed to manage this document. Accomplishing more with less doesn't have to be difficult. Sometimes it is simply a matter of using the right tool for the right job.

Calendars in SharePoint

The SharePoint calendar is not meant to replace the enterprise calendaring system. It is intended to serve as a group calendar to help schedule and manage group meetings and events. The main highlight here is the ability to create a workspace for a meeting or event. The workspace is a mini-site dedicated for this meeting or event as shown below:

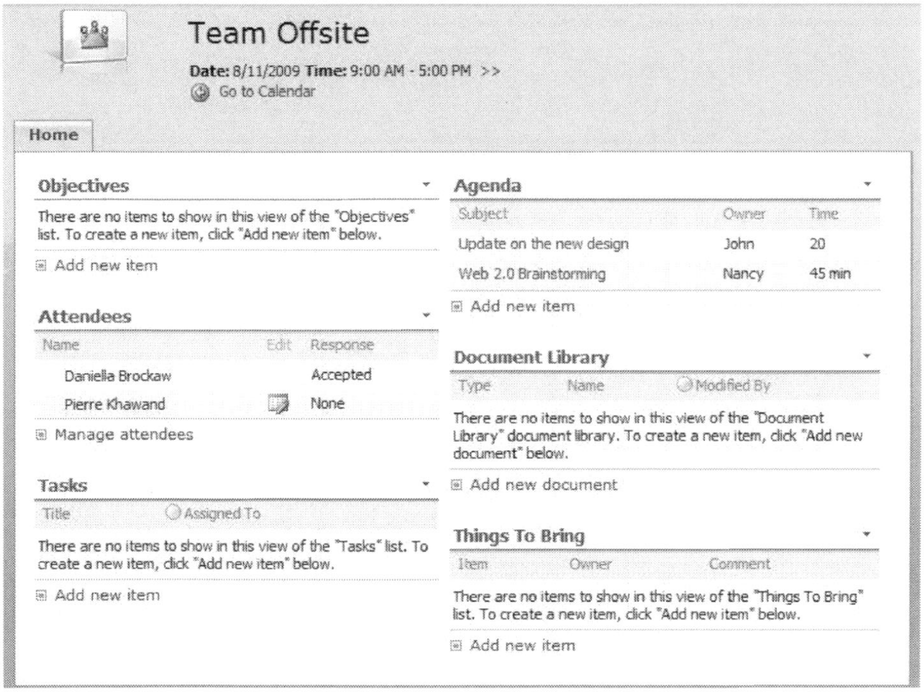

Figure 8: Meeting workspace

The team can use this workspace to prepare for the meeting, and track action items and status updates after the meeting. As mentioned in the document library discussion above, instead of having dozens of e-mails about suggested agenda items and supporting documents, we now have one "designated holding area" for this information. No confusion. No duplication of effort. No duplication of storage. This is yet another manifestation of the concept of having "designated holding areas", a concept which we discussed very early in the book when we organized the desk.

Tasks in SharePoint

When you have a group of people collaborating on a task, potentially handing over this task from one person to another when milestones are reached, sharing documents related to this task, and keeping each other updated about the progress,

SharePoint tasks can formalize this process, help define a clear workflow, and make the task easier to manage.

As an example, the marketing team created a "Collateral requests" task list in SharePoint to allow the sales team to initiate requests for sales collaterals. When a sales person sees the need for a certain sales collateral, she fills in the task request form, describes the situation and need, and potentially attaches relevant documents. She may assign the task to a product manager or to a traffic manager in the marketing team.

The product manager who has been assigned the task gets notified (see alerts below for more details) and at the next opportunity, he reviews the request and attached documents. He may then work on researching the issues, starting an outline, attaching additional resources, and then assigning the task to the copywriter who might finish their first draft and assign it back to the product manager. The sales person who initiated the request may check on the status of the task periodically and potentially provide additional input.

The home page of the marketing and sales team site can be tailored to include a list of tasks assigned to the user which is automatically displayed when the user logs in to the site.

User Tasks			
Type	Task	Item Link	Due Date
☑	Case study		8/7/2009 12:00 AM

Figure 9: User tasks shown on user's SharePoint home page

Alerts in SharePoint

SharePoint allows users to receive notifications when documents, calendars, tasks, and other items are updated by other users. For instance, you may be waiting for others to review a document that you created and provide their comments or contribute content. You can set up an alert so you get notified when users update the document. The notification will take place in the form of an e-mail which includes a link to the document.

Alerts are very flexible and powerful. For instance, we can setup alerts at the document level, or folder level, or library level. We can have alerts for certain documents, or only documents that we created, or all documents.

Podcasting

Podcasting is a mechanism that makes the publishing and distribution of audio and video files via the internet an easy process. The content can be heard and seen on desktop and laptop computers as well as mobile devices including audio players and smartphones.

Podcasts are easy to publish, easy to subscribe to, and easy to download. When a user subscribes to a podcast, which is typically done using an application such as Apple iTunes, then every time the publisher posts new content, the new content is automatically downloaded to the user's computer, and automatically added to their mobile device the next time they connect the device to the computer.

Podcasting content tends to be short and focused. Similar to blogs, the content can be private or public, personal or business. Companies use podcasts to communicate and share important information with mobile workers such as sales and field support team members. Not only can mobile workers take their content with them to customers, partners, tradeshows and conferences, but they can also get up to the minute updates when necessary. In addition, they can make use of travel time, commute time, and time that is otherwise wasted between activities.

Smartphones

Smartphones are becoming quickly and increasingly faster, more feature rich, and easier to use. In addition to phone, voice mail, and text messaging capabilities, they provide access to contacts lists, calendars, task lists, access to e-mail, chat, and the internet, as well as an extensive selection of services and add-on applications. Smartphones also provide audio and video capabilities, ranging from recording and playing audio files, taking pictures and videos, and viewing such content that is stored on the device or streaming from the internet.

Smartphones are becoming an essential productivity tool for people who are on the go. Smartphones enable mobile users to a) stay up-to-date and respond to time sensitive issues, b) share information and collaborate more easily via corporate and public internet and intranet services from anywhere at anytime, and c) take advantage of waiting time to handle e-mail, calendar, and office documents. People and companies who have deployed smartphones successfully and use them "smartly" are gaining huge advantages and accomplishing a lot more.

If you believe that smartphones would be helpful for you or your team, selecting the smartphone that best fits your needs is becoming more involved than one might think. To explore this issue of selecting a smartphone, and come up with helpful guidelines for the selection process, I have undertaken a research project in which I used 12 different smartphones for 9 days each. This included the Apple iPhone which I got on the day it was released after camping overnight outside the Apple Store in Palo Alto. While it is beyond the scope of this chapter to explore and review the smartphone selection criteria, for those interested in more information about this topic, the findings of this research were captured in a blog which was later published into "The Smartphone Experiment" book.

For those who are using smartphones or considering smartphones, here are a few relevant observations that can help get more accomplished with these devices while minimizing potential side effects:

a) Use your smartphone to stay up-to-date, handle time sensitive inquiries, but not to fully manage your e-mail and data. These management tasks are still best done on the laptop or desktop with faster Internet connection, a larger keyboard and screen, and easy access to your other documents and data.

b) Capturing notes on smartphones in meetings and during conversations is slow, can take our attention away from the people around us, and be distracting to them. If note taking is necessary, the journal may best serve this purpose. Use the journal to take notes quickly and easily while staying connected with others.

c) Aside from note taking, smartphone users can get busy checking and answering e-mail, browsing the internet, or managing their calendar at times when paying closer attention to what is going on around them could be far more valuable. Be aware of what is going on around you and give priority to the people who are present.

d) Write clear communication and do not skip the friendly greeting. With smartphones, it is easy to write short and cryptic messages, that don't make sense and appear to be unfriendly. This can cause not only confusion and wasted time and effort, but also affect working relationships. It is helpful to read your message from the receiver's point of view before sending it, and check for clarity and friendliness.

e) Don't type and drive! I invite you to make the pledge of "no typing and driving" and to promote safe use of smartphone technologies. For more information about this topic, refer to "The Smartphone Experiment" book mentioned above.

Virtual Meeting Tools—Phone, IM, Web, and Video Conferencing

Phone conferencing, instant messaging, web conferencing, and video conferencing, are likely to significantly enhance a team's ability to collaborate in real time. When a team is working collaboratively on a task or project, the ability to quickly check with someone on an issue (via instant messenger), and switch to voice if necessary (via phone conferencing), and then share screens (web conferencing), and even see each other (video conferencing), can help diagnose problems and find solutions, make decisions, leverage everyone's knowledge and all available data, brainstorm new ideas, and create compelling results in a timely and cost effective manner.

These technologies make the above possible whether two people or thousands of people are involved, and whether they are working in the same building or scattered around the globe. With these technologies, distance and time zones are "flattened" and resources are more easily pooled together. Remote workers, mobile workers, telecommuters, and people with flexible schedules, are able to stay on the same page, and get a lot accomplished.

We sometimes find resistance to these online collaboration technologies especially at organizations that have been traditionally reliant on face-to-face interactions. As these organizations grow and groups move to new locations, expand geographically and start branch offices, or start to encourage telecommuting, they are no longer able to sustain the face-to-face culture, and they have to adapt and deploy these online collaboration technologies. Those who make this transition whole heartedly and help their teams in the process quickly reap the benefits.

What about interruptions? If we have such easy access to instant messaging for instance, aren't we inviting interruptions, which can hinder our ability to focus on the task at hand? What does this do to our 40 minute of focused work? The answer is simple. When we start our focused session, we set our instant messenger status to busy or unavailable, and then when we start our collaborative session, we change it to online or available. Most importantly we work with our team to come up with agreements on how we use instant messenger to communicate to each other that we are focused, and how we escalate issues when critical issues come up.

Virtual worlds

Virtual Worlds (such as Second Life by Linden Lab) present yet another set of tools that can be used for collaboration and for improving communication and productivity. Virtual Worlds are three-dimensional online representations of real world objects (such as houses, buildings, storefronts, billboards, streets, cars) and fantasy objects (fictitious electronic gadgets, games, etc.). A user creates an avatar (a three-dimensional representation of himself or herself) and explores the virtual world content as well as communicates with other users (other avatars in the virtual world) via text chat or voice conversations. The user experience is much richer and more engaging than the traditional audio and web conferencing tools. In addition to serving as social and commerce platforms for individuals and retailers, Virtual Worlds enable business users to communicate effectively, organize virtual meetings and events, host employee orientation and training programs, and design and test product concepts before actual productions in the real world, among other things.

Figure 10: One of the People-OnTheGo training rooms in Second Life

Business and Social Networking

Business and social networking sites enable users to connect with business colleagues and personal friends easily, stay connected over time as people change jobs and locations, and leverage each other's knowledge and resources. Most of these sites allow users to form groups around common interests. When you become a member of a group, you typically gain access to group resources and become automatically connected with the group members. With hundreds of millions of users, these networks are becoming a primary target for businesses that want to market and sell their products and services. Here is an overview of three of the most popular platforms.

LinkedIn in a nutshell

LinkedIn is one of the most popular business networking sites with millions of users (the number grows daily) and a constantly evolving feature set. Recruiters and job seekers alike use LinkedIn as a recruiting and job search platform. If you are looking for a job, or keeping an eye on your career development, or seeking talent for your team or company, being active in LinkedIn is now considered a must. This also means having a well written and up-to-date LinkedIn profile with endorsements from colleagues, bosses, customers, partners, and even vendors.

LinkedIn supports the group functionality described above. LinkedIn also allows users to post questions relating to any business issue that they are dealing with, and get answers from other LinkedIn users. This provides the user who is asking a question with valuable information, and the user who is answering a question an opportunity to highlight their expertise. LinkedIn also introduced the "applications" features making it easier to have add-on functionality and extend the functionality of the system.

Facebook in a nutshell

Facebook is one of the most popular social networking sites with several hundred millions users. While Facebook started as a platform for college graduates to connect with each other, it has grown to be the social networking platform of choice for users of all ages including corporate users.

Facebook is also an application development platform. It allows users to develop applications and then make them available to the Facebook community. Users can then share these applications with other users creating a very powerful virtual marketing phenomenon. This makes the platform very attractive to companies who have products and services to promote. Facebook is targeting these companies with capabilities such as allowing them to create web pages on Facebook, and to easily tap into the online advertisement and market research capabilities that the platform provides.

Twitter in a nutshell

Twitter is also called the micro-blogging platform. It enables users to send and receive messages up to 140 characters (referred to as tweets). Tweets are displayed on the author's profile page and are only visible to users who are connected with the author (these users are also called "followers"). Twitter has gained a lot of popularity worldwide and it has emerged as the primary platform for getting the most up-to-date information (informal) about news and events worldwide – including what is being said in conferences and presentations the moment that it is said.

Action Plan

Identify the action items that you would like to take as a result of what was covered in this chapter. Indicate the timeframe in which you plan on taking these actions. Then report on the actual date in which you implemented them and a brief note about the results.

Table 4: Action Plan

Practice/Technique	I will start implementing this on (date?)	Actual start date	Actual end date	Comment/Results
Using a blog				
Using a wiki				
Using Microsoft SharePoint				
Using Podcasting and VodCasting				
Using Smartphones				
Using Virtual Meeting Tools				
Learning/experimenting with Virtual Worlds				
Using Social Networking platforms				
Add your own item:				
Add your own item:				
Add your own item:				

Chapter 12: All wishful thinking until we take action

It is all wishful thinking until we take action. A lot happens when we take action! We discover and learn. We challenge the mind and the irrational beliefs that it holds on to. We set more constructive precedence for the future.

Why don't we take action?

If we know what to do, why don't we do it? Most of the time, we know what to do, but we still don't do it. Or we are capable of figuring out what to do, but we still don't put forth the necessary effort to figure it out. Scott Peck, the author of the Road Less Traveled, mentions laziness, fear, and pride, as the root causes of many of our troubles. I argue that they are the root causes behind our hesitation in taking action.

The paradox is that taking action helps dissolve laziness, uncover and dismantle our irrational beliefs behind the fear, and soften our pride. This is the "chicken and egg" theory. So how do we get started? How do we overcome the initial fear, laziness, and pride that is stopping us from getting the action started in the first place? Here are some ways we can get started:

1. Journaling about the action, and the reasons why the action is desirable, and what benefit it will bring.
2. Journaling about the irrational beliefs that may be preventing us from moving forward, disputing them, and formulating more rational and realistic views.
3. Visualizing and role playing in a safe environment.
4. Identifying small steps we can take to get started.
5. Finding a support system ranging from helpful resources to supportive friends and colleagues, to getting the help of a professional coach.
6. In some cases, it may be "just doing it" and challenging the laziness, fear, and pride. This involves tolerating the discomfort, only to find out soon, that the discomfort quickly goes away.

Turning the Accomplishing-more-with-less concepts and techniques into action

If you have already identified the actions that you want to take as a result of the Accomplishing-more-with-less methodology by filling out your action plan at the end of each chapter, then formulating your final action plan below should be easy. If not, this is your opportunity to reflect on what you learned and come up with your action plan now.

Start with 3 easy actions or practices that you can implement right away, and one more challenging action or practice that is likely to take more planning and more implementation time. The 3 easy actions will give you some immediate benefits and get you motivated to do more. The more challenging action will give you more significant and sustainable results.

There are plenty of actions to choose from. Here is a list of what some of our workshop participants selected as their three easy actions or practices:

- Use e-mail flags to manage unfinished messages.

- Set up a catch-all e-mail folder.

- Start using the journal.

- Start the beginning of day reconciliation at the beginning of each day.

- Start the end of day reconciliation at the end of each day.

- Set up a catch-all to-do list.

- Work in 40 minute focused sessions followed by collaborative sessions.

- Get a timer and use it to stay focused during the focused sessions.

- Starting micro-planning when working on an important task.

- Turn off the e-mail beep when new messages arrive.

- Incorporate purposeful breaks after each collaborative session and before the next focused session.

- Use the Immediate Priorities Matrix™ when you have many conflicting priorities, or every two weeks to plan more effectively.

Here are some examples of more challenging items that some of our workshop participants have chosen:

- Organize the filing structure and start using the new structure.

- Organize the desk.

- Empty the e-mail inbox.

- Negotiate with your team/boss/and other group members how to communicate to each other that you are focused and how to escalate issues when issues come up.

- Use the End Results Matrix™ to identify the desired results for the next 3 to 6 months and then work at incorporating these activities into the schedule.

- Identify specific high-impact activities (that are part of the 20% effort that is bringing 80% of the results) and incorporate more of these activities into your schedule.

- Identify specific low-impact activities (that are part of the 80% effort that is only bringing minimal results) and do less of these activities.

- Select a difficult work or personal situation that is taking up a lot of time and energy, and using stress management techniques to identify the best possible action.

- Engage in further training and/or coaching activities to develop specific skills that will help accelerate your development.

Once you complete the above action plan, you will be motivated to take on the next step of actions, and this is the beginning of a whole new journey of growth, development, and accomplishment. Congratulations for having chosen this path!

Your Accomplishing more with less Action Plan

Table 21: Identify someone who can support you in this process (your informal coach)

Name	
E-mail	
Phone	

Table 22: List the three easy items, and dates you will get them done by

1.		
2.		
3.		

Table 23: List the more challenging item, and date you will get it done by

1.		
	Date/time on which you will spend 30 to 40 minutes to plan how you will get this done	

Your implementation checklist

- ☐ I executed the three easy items.
- ☐ I e-mailed my "coach" about having completed the three easy items.
- ☐ I scheduled my 30 to 40 minute session to plan my challenging item.
- ☐ I e-mailed my "coach" about my challenging item.
- ☐ I accomplished my challenging item.
- ☐ And don't forget to make use of the gift certificate that is provided to you with this workbook (see the introduction at the beginning of the workbook for the more details).

Date completed _____